THE Job Hunter's Catalog

By Peggy Schmidt

Design: Dorit Tabak

Illustrations: Chris Kalb

T0339052

JOHN WILEY & SONS, INC.
New York • Chichester • Brisbane • Toronto • Singapore

To Nancy Riggs Jones,
a gifted teacher and writer

Schmidt, Peggy J.
The job hunter's catalog/ Peggy Schmidt.
p.   cm.
Includes bibliographical references.
ISBN 0-471-04733-3 (cloth)   ISBN 0-471-04731-7 (paper)
1. Job hunting—Handbooks, manuals, etc. 2. Vocational guidance—Handbooks, manuals, etc. I. Title HF5382.7.S36 1995 650.14—dc20 95-13625CIP

Printed in the United States of America

10 9 8 7 6 5 4 3 2 1

CONTENTS

ABOUT THE AUTHOR

Peggy Schmidt has written hundreds of articles on careers, education and job search strategies for national publications, including the *New York Times, Child, Working Woman, Glamour, First for Women* and *New Woman*. Her syndicated column, "Your New Job," has been carried in the (New York) *Daily News,* the *Boston Herald,* the *Oakland Tribune,* and the *Atlanta Journal-Constitution*. Her books include: *The 90 Minute Resume* (Peterson's); *Making It Big in the City: A Woman's Guide to Living, Loving and Working There* (McGraw Hill); and *Making It On Your First Job* (Avon Books). She produced the *Careers Without College* 14-book series for Peterson's. She currently serves as West Coast Director of the American Book Producers Association and is a program chair of the Electronic Publishing SIG of the San Francisco chapter of the IICS. She can be reached at: 73107,3604 (CompuServe) or PeggyNCC@aol.com.

ABOUT THE DESIGNER

Dorit Tabak has been creating print materials for a variety of organizations and products for over fifteen years. Those include marketing brochures, annual reports, catalogs, corporate identity programs, fund raising and special event packages and direct mail campaigns. This is her first book design. Tabak Design's award–winning work has been exhibited in the Creativity Show, the Association of Graphic Arts and the Art Director's Club. Dorit can be reached at TabakD@aol.com.

ABOUT THE ILLUSTRATOR

Chris Kalb designed and illustrated *Tray Gourmet: Be Your Own Chef in the College Cafeteria* (Lake Isle Press) and *The On-Track Trainer: Training in the Hospitality Industry* (Cornell Hotel School). He has also illustrated *Up Your S.A.T. Score* (Workman) *'Scuse Me While I Kiss This Guy* (Fireside), and designed *Low-Fat Living for Real People* (Lake Isle Press). Chris's comic strip in *The Yale Daily News* won him Scripps-Howard's Charles M. Schulz Award for the nation's most promising college cartoonist. Chris has begun to fulfill that promise by winning a 1993 Suburban Newspapers of America Award for his weekly editorial cartoon. His cartoons appear in the suburban Philadelphia weekly Montgomery Newspapers, where Chris also served as head designer.

ACKNOWLEDGMENTS

I deeply appreciate the advice, ideas, and suggestions of the following people in writing this book.

Bill Aberman, chairman of BPI, which organizes job fairs

John Albach, Director of the National Stuttering Project, 2151 Irving Street, Suite 208, San Francisco, CA 94122-1609 or call: 1-800-364-1677

Nella Barkley, president of Crystal/Barkley Corporation, New York City-based consultants on productivity and career planning issues

Will Cantrell, editor and publisher of the monthly newsletter, International Employment Hotline , P.O. Box 3030, Oakton, Virginia 22124-9030, 703-620-1972

Charlotte Chapman, a certified addictions counselor in private practice and chair of the ethics committee of the National Association of Alcoholism and Drug Abuse Counselors

Dobisky Associations, a college media relations firm in Keene, New Hampshire

Beatrice Dohrn, legal director of the Lambda Legal Defense and Education Fund, a national organization based in New York City

Scott Ehrenpreiss, a C.P.A. with Becker and Co. in New York City

John D. Erdlen, president of Strategic Outsourcing, Inc. in Wellesley and Boston, Massachusetts

David Fram, policy attorney in the Americans with Disabilities Act divison of the Equal Employment Opportunity Commission in Washington, D.C.

Al Geoghegan, a retired financial account executive for the Wall Street Journal and coordinator of four job clubs in Pennsylvania and New York

Jon P. Goodman, Ph.D., director of the Entrepeneur Program at the University of Southern California

Dr. Joel Goodman, Ed.D., founder of The Humor Project, Dept. YNJ, 110 Spring St., Saratoga Springs, New York 12866, 518-587-8770

Susan Gordon, vice president, the Lynne Palmer Agency, which specializes in the publishing industry

Rhoda Frindell Green, Ph.D., a New York City-based psychological consultant specializing in career planning and development

Dr. Mardy Grothe, a psychologist and management consultant with Performance Improvement Associates, based in Washington, D.C. and Boston

v

Dr. Sandra Haber, Ph.D., a clinical psychologist in New York City and a stress expert

Jeannine Harrold, Director of Career Services at Ball State University, Muncie, Indiana

Dr. Charles Hennon, a Miami University professor and editor of the journal *Lifestyles: Family and Economic Issues*

Tom Jackson, author of *The Perfect Resume* and other books, and chairman of Equinox, a human resources management and training firm in New York City

Maria Laqueur, president of the American Association of Part-Time Professionals in Falls Church, Virginia

David Larson, professor of labor law and employment discrimination at Creighton University School of Law, Omaha, Nebraska

James Levine, director of the Fatherhood Project at the Work and Family Insitute, a nonprofit research institution in New York City

Darien McWhirter, a lawyer and author of *Your Rights At Work*

David Mitcham, a corporate manager for employment practices who wrote *The Reference Checking Handbook* published by the American Society for Personnel Administration, a professional organization in Washington, D.C.

Charles Shanor, a professor of law at Emory University, Atlanta, Georgia and formerly general counsel to the Equal Employment Opportunity Commission

Elayne Snyder, a New York City-based speech consultant and author of the book, *Persuasive Business Speaking*

James Stanislaw, a tax attorney with Keating, McPencow & Stanislaw in San Francisco

Bill Torchiana, president of Torchiana, Mastrov & Associates, an outplacement consulting firm in San Francisco

Dr. Stanley Weingart, Ph.D., a psychologist who specializes in stress management and teaches at the University of Southern California School of Business Administration

Suzanne West, a Palo Alto-based graphic designer and author of *Working With Style: Traditional and Modern Approaches to Layout and Typography*

Neil M. Yeager, Ed.D., a recruiter with Charter Oaks in Hartford, Connecticut, and co-author of the book *Power Interviews*

Dr. Baila Zeitz, Ph.D. a New York City-based psychologist and an expert on career and family issues

WHAT'S IN THIS BOOK

Page through this book and you will see that it looks different from most of the other titles on this shelf. It's a collection of job-hunting ideas, each catalogued by topic, that are the result of my twenty-plus years of writing about and advising people on how to go about finding the right job. We—the book's designer, illustrator, and I—have tried to make this information reader-friendly and accessible by using headlines and icons to help you find the information you're looking for. We have also used illustrations to help make a point or make you smile.

Because *The Job Hunter's Catalog* is not written in the linear fashion of most books, it's up to you to select what you want to read and when. Its organization does resemble a job hunt start to finish, but you might want to browse through the last chapter, Special Problems, first to find out if one of the stories there is likely to speak to your needs. Or you may want to start with Chapter 2, The Resume and Cover Letter, to get ideas on how to make yours the best they can be. The bottom line is that the book is designed so that you can decide what is likely to interest and help you most in your job search. If something isn't relevant to your situation, you can skip it and not feel that you're missing out on something.

Many of the situations and problems I have addressed in this book have been sent to me over the years by readers of my job column, which has appeared in the *New York Daily News,* the *Oakland Tribune,* the *Boston Herald,* and the *Atlanta Journal-Constitution.* I'm indebted to them for sharing their stories, and I hope you find the suggestions I've passed along to them (many of which come from experts who are listed in the Acknowledgments section) to be helpful.

As a collector of both job-hunting tales and advice from experts, I believe there is an art to looking for and finding a job that is satisfying. It's something that some people do well without much coaching because they're compulsive about identifying job openings, and get offers because they come across well in person (in addition, of course, to being qualified for the job). But most of us need reminders of things we ought to be doing to locate job openings and suggestions on how we can dress, behave and speak more convincingly in a job interview. This book is full of thoughtful ideas, many of which have been passed along to me from headhunters, college placement directors, recruiters, and interviewers.

One of the most embarrassing but instructional things that ever happened to me during a job search (my first one after college) was having an employment agency counselor chide me for having not washed my hands before the interview. I had been reading the morning paper and the newsprint had indeed smudged my hands. I was so taken aback by her candor that I was speechless. I never showed up again with hands that looked like they belonged to Cinderella.

The point of this parable is that advice given person-to-person can be devastating, particularly if it's from someone you hope will hire you. It's far better to do a self checklist of things you may be doing, saying or omitting that can hurt your chances of getting a job. This book will provide you with the plenty of lists and questions so that you can do just that (and save yourself embarrassment or rejection).

Because looking for a job is an art, not a game in which there are set rules, you may find that giving the advice in this book your own "twist" is the way to go, both for your own comfort and success. I encourage you to adapt those strategies that fit your style and personality and modify those that do not. If you take the advice in the book's pages to heart, however, I can assure you that you will be a savvier job hunter whose chances of landing a job you really want are better than ever.

                              Peggy Schmidt
                              June, 1995

CHAPTER 1

JOB SEARCH PRELIMINARIES

YOUR BOSS IS LEAVING: SHOULD YOU START JOB HUNTING?

The news that your boss is leaving his or her position can be as traumatic as the breakup of a romantic relationship if the two of you get along well. Even if you don't, his departure will prompt you to wonder how it will affect you. Because new bosses are often given the leeway to hire new staff or the mandate to cut costs, your job could be in jeopardy. Here are the factors most likely to influence whether you should start looking for a new job.

● The circumstances under which your boss left. If her departure was not of her own choosing, chances are changes could be in the wind for you and other staff members. If you are on good terms with your boss, find out as much as she's willing to tell you about why she was given her walking papers. If you are friendly with someone else on her level or higher, that person could be as good, if not better, a source

of information about what the future holds for you.

If you discover that cutbacks are in the offing or that a reorganization is underway, it's smart to update your resume. If, on the other hand, your boss was fired for poor performance, it's probably not necessary to start reading the help wanted ads unless you were considered your boss's protégé.

● How top management views you. The better known you have been to people at your boss's level or above, the better your chances of being kept on— provided their assessments of your work performance are good. It's not too late, though, to make your accomplishments known. Your best bet is to write a short letter to your boss's boss, a top manager with whom you are acquainted, or the head of personnel listing your accomplishments and skills you feel are most useful to your company. Let the person know that you are flexible and would consider moving to another department.

● Company style. Look at what's happened in the past as an indicator of what's likely to happen to you. If, for example, the most junior staff members are kept on when a department head leaves but higher-level staff are often let go, you can get a handle on your fate. You cannot, however, use past history as a guide if your company has undergone a merger or a takeover.

● Your adaptability. If you can go with the flow, and view change and new situations as a challenge rather than a threat, you should give the new boss a try. He or she may want you to adjust the way you've been doing things to better suit his or her work style. If you're open to new ideas and don't mind tinkering with your routine, your flexibility can work to your advantage.

If, on the other hand, you feel loyal to your boss who is leaving under less than wonderful circumstances and feel you may take out your resentment on the new boss (consciously or unconsciously), put your feelers out into the job market. You won't last if your feelings affect your job performance, and you will probably be happier with a new job and a boss of your choosing.

● How satisfied you are with your job. Liking your work counts for a lot; it can mean the critical difference in making a successful transition to a new boss. And don't discount the possibility that your job responsibilities, status, or salary may grow if your new boss is the type who likes to empower the people who work for him. If, however, you have stuck with your job because it's a comfortable routine, not because you really enjoy the work, this may be the right time to reassess what makes you happy and go looking for that opportunity.

● Your financial situation. Even if your best instincts tell you it may be time to go, you may not be able to comfortably manage a change right now. If that's the case, go out of your way to prove to your new boss that you're an invaluable member of the staff. Doing so will allow you to conduct a job search in a time frame you can control.

● Your marketability. If your chances of finding a comparable or better job are good, you stand to lose little by taking a look around. You may discover that you are worth more than you think, or find out that you can comfortably move up a notch or two in your career. That information alone can help prepare you to negotiate with your current employer if he wants you to stay—or cushion the news that the new boss is eliminating your position or replacing you.□

5
●

HOW TO DETERMINE YOUR MARKETABILITY AND WORTH

Unless you know what your skills and experience are worth in today's job market, you may shortchange yourself. Here's how to evaluate them:

SALARY Check with people you know or have worked with about the salary range their companies are paying for a job such as yours. Then dig deeper. Salary surveys are often published annually by magazines such as *Working Woman* (January issue) and in publications for professionals in specific fields. The *Occupational Outlook Handbook* (published by the U.S. Department of Labor Statistics) uses many salary sources to come up with paycheck information in specific fields. You can find that publication in your local library.

Help wanted advertisements sometimes provide salary ranges that can be helpful. Another check is to visit a reputable employment agency, preferably one that specializes in placing people in your field. After reviewing your resume, an experienced placement counselor should be able to tell you what salary range you might expect. Some major agencies, such as Source Edp (which helps place people with computer, data management and engineering skills), publish annual salary surveys. Keep in mind that the most important determinant of salary is whether people with your credentials are in demand.

EXPERIENCE It's sometimes difficult to know if you have been given the level of responsibility and status your experience warrants, particularly if you have been working for the same employer for a number of years. A rough gauge of whether your position matches your experience is to look at the experience required in jobs at a higher level than yours in the help wanted ads.

An experienced counselor at an employment agency can also give you an idea of the job level you should go for. Comparing notes with others in your field through a local business group or professional association can also help you get a handle on what to look for.

SKILLS In fields where familiarity with computers or other technologies are critical to doing a good job, the most important question is whether your skills are state-of the-art. If they're not, taking a course or certificate program may determine whether you'll be seriously considered as a candidate.

PERSONABLENESS Being perceived as a team player is an important factor in any hiring decision, although there is no objective measure of what this factor is worth. If you feel your ability to get along with others is one of your strong points, you can bring it up in interviews and ask your references to be sure to talk about it when prospective employers contact them.□

IMPROVE YOUR WRITING SKILLS

Knowing how to put together a clear, concise sentence is essential to doing almost any job. If you are not confident about how well you communicate on paper, it's to your advantage to invest time improving your writing skills. And how well you write may be a factor in how quickly you move up.

Many adult education divisions of high schools and community colleges offer low-cost writing courses (as little as $3 per instruction hour). You might want to take one that emphasizes business writing—business letters, memos, and short reports. On the other hand, any course that required you to practice the skill and provided instructor feedback would be valuable.

If you are the kind of learner who is highly self-motivated, visit your local library or bookstore and get copies of classic writing how-to-write books, such as *Simple and Direct* by Jacques Barzun or *On Writing Well*, by William Zinsser.

Finally, the secret to improving your writing skills is to write and revise. If you go the self-help route, be sure to let someone who is a good writer point out grammatical errors, awkward sentence constructions, and unclear or imprecise language.□

Q & A

WHEN YOU HAVE NO RELATED JOB EXPERIENCE

Q: I graduated last June and spent the summer working in the job I've had for the last four years—waitressing. Now that I'm job hunting, I keep getting the same message from employers: "You don't have any experience in this field." How can I persuade them to give me a chance?

A: The Catch-22 you're encountering is a common one, but you cannot afford to let it discourage you. One strategy is to go on the offensive: Before an employer can make the statement, address the issue yourself. Say that while you do not have experience doing that particular kind of work, you have gained valuable on-the-job experience that you feel will help you be an ace employee. Then mention at least three skills or qualities that you think will be particularly attractive to the employer—your ability to learn routines quickly, your familiarity with software or computer systems, your ability to deal with customers. Give examples of each, and, if possible, try to talk about how these skills can be transferred to the industry you're trying to get into.□

MAKING A PROFESSIONAL VOICEMAIL MESSAGE

Here's how to create a good first impression with your phone message:

DO write a short, to-the-point script. You can simply say, "Hello, this is (your name). Unfortunately, I cannot take your call just now, but if you would leave your name, number, and a time when it would be convenient for me to reach you, I'll try to call you then."

DO practice saying your script. It should not sound as if it's being read. Speak slowly and clearly, and work at sounding friendly.

DON'T play any background music. It's more appropriate for a recorded message that's intended for family and friends.

DO warn the caller if there is a long gap between the time your recorded message ends and the proverbial "beep," or if they cannot begin recording until the long beep, so they don't hang up or begin speaking prematurely.

DON'T laugh, cough, or sound hesitant or flip.□

NEGOTIATE UNDERSTANDING BEFORE INTERNSHIP BEGINS

In some fields, particularly nonprofit and artistic fields, working as an unpaid intern has traditionally been an acceptable way to break in. Before you agree to such an arrangement, make sure you really want to work for a particular employer or feel the experience you can get will help you land a job elsewhere. Investigate whether others who have gone this route with a particular employer have been hired after proving their worth. Finally, negotiate:

- The hours you are expected to work
- Who you will report to
- What your specific responsibilities will be
- How long it will be before he or she will decide whether to formally hire you
- Nonmonetary perks you can get as an intern
- Formal or informal training you will receive
- A letter of recommendation if a job isn't forthcoming and you decide to leave.□

SHOULD YOU GO INTO BUSINESS FOR YOURSELF INSTEAD OF LOOKING FOR ANOTHER JOB?

Many job hunters flirt with the idea of going into business for themselves. Coming up with what you think is a great idea is only the first step; if you're serious, take the following steps:

1. Determine whether you have skills or experience that can work in a small business. The most likely success stories are businesses: (1) based on a need identified by someone with experience in a particular field or industry or (2) in which the entrepreneur has an expertise that's not widely available but in demand.

If, in your current or previous job, there was one product you needed but could not get or a service that would have expedited work but that was unavailable, you may have the germ of a good business idea. Increasingly, big companies are relying on small ones to take care of tasks they can no longer afford to do on the inside, whether it's electronic services, paper destruction, or account servicing.

If you are someone with a technical skill that's in demand or you have a new idea on how to use that skill to meet a consumer need, you are also starting on firm footing. For example, computer and office repair technicians who are on call to homes and businesses have often succeeded as entrepreneurs.

2. Put your idea in writing. Doing so will compel you to define and refine your thinking. First, try to express your idea in a succinct sentence or two. Then flesh it out by setting up categories such as: The Market for My Product or Service; The Competition; What a Start-Up Will Require (equipment, work space, personnel, inventory, etc.); Skills/Expertise Needed (your own or those of others).

3. Research your idea. Your first stop should be the business reference section of your local library. Ask the librarian

for help in finding out everything you can about starting a business in the field you have targeted, and the facts about doing business in your area and state.

4. Contact your Chamber of Commerce. Active ones conduct seminars on new business startups, do one-on-one counseling, and are willing to introduce you to more established business people who are their members.

5. Talk to everyone you can about their reactions to your plan. Don't be hesitant about revealing your idea for fear it will be stolen; ideas are a dime a dozen—implementing one is hard work. (The exception to this rule: sharing it with a company already in the same business.)

6. Estimate how much it will cost to launch your business. Use two equations when figuring out how much money you will need: (1) how much capital you need for supplies, equipment, rent, and telephones; and (2) how long it will take before you see your first revenue. Double that time (it always takes longer than you think), and calculate how much money you will need to maintain your present lifestyle. While it's fine to ballpark prices if you're familiar with going rates, don't blue sky them. If necessary, call vendors or people who rent office space, provide services, or supply temporary personnel to get a realistic idea of what your costs are likely to be. Don't expect to get money from banks or venture capital firms. Most new business startups are cookie-jar financed; that is, the money comes from your savings or that of friends or relatives. If your cookie jar is not full enough, consider moonlighting your business startup while you work full time.

7. Analyze all the reasons why your business may fail. Sure, you should think positive, but many new businesses do not survive for long, often because entrepreneurs fail to plan ahead for the unexpected. You are more likely to succeed if you anticipate problems, and come up with alternative approaches to solving them.□

THINK CAREFULLY ABOUT RELOCATING

The more flexible you are about where you will work, the better your chances of finding the job you want. But be sure to ask yourself these hard questions before you start broadening your job search:

1. CAN YOU SWING A MOVE FINANCIALLY?

Find out what it's going to cost you to live in the new area. Housing is the single most expensive item, and you have to factor in the cost of selling your present home (if you are a homeowner) and buying a new one in a similar neighborhood. If you rent, compare rental costs. Factor in the costs of moving your belongings, too.

2. CAN YOU SEE YOURSELF LIVING IN THE AREA WHERE YOU INTEND TO LOOK FOR A JOB?

Because your satisfaction with your personal life affects your job performance, find out what the cultural, recreational, educational, and social opportunities are ahead of time.

3. HOW IS YOUR SPOUSE OR FAMILY GOING TO REACT?

If your partner is working, investigate how easy it will be for him or her to find a similar job elsewhere. Moving away from relatives can be traumatic, too, not just for your spouse but for your children. Changing schools, leaving friends, and giving up activities can deeply affect their happiness. Making the decision to look for a job in a new place is likely to work out for the best if it's a joint or family venture. If you talk to them before you decide, you may be able to allay their fears.□

CAREER COUNSELORS CAN HELP

If you aren't sure what your next move should be, working with a career counselor may be a smart investment. To find a good one, ask friends and colleagues for suggestions, or contact the career placement office of a local college. Their staff often does one-on-one counseling. Another source: the job information services division of major libraries. Some offer free counseling by appointment; others may be able to refer you to counselors.

Before you agree to start working with a counselor, be sure to ask:

1. What are the counselor's credentials? A graduate degree in counseling or in a social science field such as social work, human services, or psychology is a plus. If she has done counseling as part of her training, it's an additional indication of her competence.

Another indication of professionalism is whether the counselor is certified by the National Career Development Association, which requires a graduate degree in counseling or a related field, completion of supervised counseling experience, at least three years full-time work experience in the field, and passing a written examination.

2. Who are the counselor's clients? Find out how closely their backgrounds and problems parallel yours. If,

for example, the counselor has worked extensively with students and you have years of work experience, it may not be the best match.

3. What can you do for me? Briefly describe your career quandary and have the counselor suggest what services he feels are most appropriate. These might include individual or group counseling, testing, and exercises to improve decision-making or job-hunting skills. If you have a "where do I go from here?"-type career problem, the experienced counselor will want to gather all kinds of information about you—your interests, aptitudes, skills, values, and goals—before beginning the career planning process.

4. How much will it cost? Compare the fees of several counselors to get an idea of what the going rate is. Be wary of anyone who insists on charging you for a package of services. Make sure that you can stop at any time if you are not satisfied, and that you will only be expected to pay for services already provided.

Beware of counselors who make promises of more money, a better job, or immediate solutions to your career dilemma. The best any good counselor can do is provide you with the tools to make your own decisions, and help you figure out strategies to implement them.□

DO YOU NEED TO CHANGE GEARS OR JOBS?

Do you feel like you have a case of the Monday morning blues every day at work? If you do, realize that leaving your job may not be the only or best solution. It's possible that you may be able to recapture your enthusiasm by working with your boss to redefine your job. Here's how:

● Analyze which tasks you are happiest doing at work or in an "extracurricular" activity. You may have done them at one time but found it necessary to delegate them as you moved up; or you may enjoy certain tasks that occur less frequently than you would like. On the other hand, if a nonwork activity was most satisfying, look into how the skills involved in doing it successfully could be transferred into your present work situation.

● Review the conditions surrounding your enjoyment of past work or non-work activity—the physical environment, the people you interacted with, the travel involved. Try to come up with ideas on how you can integrate those same conditions into your current work situation.

● Investigate your options. Once you come to grips with the kind of work you most want to do, determine whether you might be able to apply those skills in your department or company. Figure out how your skills might specifically solve a problem or help your company.

If, for example, you are a secretary who wants to spend more time doing events planning (a function now shared by several people), come up with a proposal for why it could be more effectively and successfully done by one person—you. Try to anticipate your boss's objections in advance so that you can effectively counter them.

● Talk to your boss or the person who has the power to implement your proposal. Make your pitch verbally, but prepare a written copy to leave behind.

● Realize that your boss might find it impossible to implement your request because of economic or other forces beyond his or her control (the ones you don't know about may also flaw your proposal). If that's the case, be prepared to consider other alternatives, including:

A lateral move within your company. The pluses: It can broaden your experience, make you more promotable, and offer new challenges, and, if you're a valued employee, it's much easier than looking for a new job on the outside. The minuses: A salary increase is improbable, and you may have to report to someone with less experience than you.

A similar position with a new company in the same industry. The pluses: It's an opportunity to choose a corporate culture closer to your own values, and there is the potential for a salary increase or improved benefits and the possibility of better future positions. The minuses: The grind of hunting for a new job and the new job stress of proving your worth to a new employer.

A similar position in a different industry. The pluses: The opportunity to learn a new, more interesting business and the groundwork for wider future job options. The minuses: A more protracted job hunt and the possibility of a salary decrease.

A career change. The pluses: It can restore the thrill of working, a sense of being in control, and the challenge of new beginnings. The minuses: It may take a while for you to get the education or retraining you need to break in, and involve a loss of income and a feeling of being "old" relative to your colleagues.□

JOB HUNT STARTING POINT: YOUR PUBLIC LIBRARY

Thinking of changing career fields? Interested in identifying employers you hadn't thought of? Need information about where to get career counseling? Free information and advice is available at your nearest public library, which offers the following resources and services. (College students can often find the same information and services in their school library or the campus career planning and placement office.)

PRINTED INFORMATION

The written word is every library's mainstay, and you will find plenty of books and pamphlets about changing careers, job search techniques, and resume writing as well as information about specific career areas. Since some may be part of the reference collection (and cannot be checked out), be sure to bring pencil and paper (or portable computer or scanner).

Directories that identify employers and list their products and services, addresses, telephone numbers, and even division heads are also available. Some of the best such general references include:

- *Hoover's Handbook of American Business, 1995: Profiles of Over 500 Major*

U.S. Companies, Fifth Edition (Reference Press).

- *Job Seeker's Guide to Private and Public Companies* (Gale Research).

- *Million Dollar Directory* (Dun & Bradstreet Information Services). Volume 3 lists businesses geographically.

- *Standard & Poor's Register of Corporations, Directors, and Executives.* Volume 2 lists companies by location.

- *The National Directory of Addresses and Phone Numbers* (Gale Research).

There are also directories that are specific to certain geographic areas or fields.

DATABASES

If you want to develop a list of prospective employers or locate articles about a particular company or business trend, you may be able to access information by using a computer and tapping into databases on CD-ROM, including *Business Index* (Public Edition), *ABI/Inform* and *General BusinessFile,* which offers Company ProFile. A library that serves a large number of users may also have telephone lines set up to its computers so that librarians can search databases online, which means communicating with a computer at another location. You may have to pay for an online search since database vendors often charge a per-minute fee for accessing their information files, so be sure to find out what the costs may

be before you order a search. *The Business Periodicals Index, The New York Times Index* and *The Wall Street Journal Index* are available as reference books or on CD-ROM.

COMPUTER-BASED CAREER COUNSELING

If you are not sure whether you want to stay in your current field or are undecided about the type of career to pursue, you can get a software career decision-making program. The two that are most widely available are "SIGI Plus," developed by the Educational Testing Service, and "Discover," developed by the American College Testing Program. No keyboard or computer skills are needed to use either program.

REFERRALS

Librarians may be able to refer you to agencies that offer career counseling and workshops. Some libraries post county and other job openings.

HELP WANTED ADS

If you plan to look for a job in another geographic area, you can peruse the classified job sections from major metropolitan newspapers in the periodicals or newspaper room of your library. The library may also carry back issues of the *National Business Employment Weekly,* and *Job Ads USA,* which is a compilation of job listings from newspapers nationwide. □

"TEMP" WORK: NOT JUST A PAYCHECK

If you have had trouble finding a full-time job or cannot work full time, consider signing up with a temporary service. You can accept assignments where and when you want to, which is especially attractive to people in the arts whose work is not regular, those in-between jobs, parents, and students. If you are undecided about your career or trying to break into a particular field full time, temping can help you make a decision or even lead to a full-time position.

HOW TEMPORARY SERVICES WORK

Client businesses contact temporary services when they need additional personnel to help during peak periods, replace vacationing or sick employees, or work on special projects. The temporary service then gets in touch with you to find out if you are available to take on the assignment, which may be as short as a half-day or as long as several months. You are paid by the temporary service on a weekly basis for the hours you have worked. While temporaries often work traditional nine-to-five workdays, some are asked to work evening, graveyard (midnight to early morning), or weekend hours.

WHO THEY NEED

People with good office skills, particularly with expertise in word processing, desktop publishing, graphics, database management, and spreadsheet software, are in demand. Many temporary services are also willing to cross-train you on word processing programs; the more of these you are familiar with, the greater the number of assignments you will be able to choose from. You may, however, be required to work as a temp for that service a certain number of hours before you are allowed to undergo training.

Generally speaking, the more skills you have, the higher your hourly rate. Certified public accountants can earn more than accountants, who earn more than bookkeepers, for example. Likewise, you may be able to up your earnings if you are bilingual.

Professionals in fields ranging from library science to public relations to management information systems are increasingly in demand at temporary services that specialize in placing employees in one or more related fields.

FINDING THE RIGHT AGENCY

The best place to start is with the help wanted section of the newspaper, because that's where services who are actively recruiting employees can be found. The *Yellow Pages* can help you identify agencies specializing in a particular industry or field.

Make an appointment with your top choice services over the phone. Be prepared to take tests measuring your office skills if you are applying for a bookkeeping, clerical, or secretarial position. You will also be interviewed, asked to provide references, and show identification and evidence of your eligibility to work in the United States.

It's smart to interview with several services before deciding which one is right for you. How you are treated as a temp applicant is an important barometer of what working with that service will be like. If the reception isn't courteous or professional, look elsewhere. Shop around for the best hourly rate for your services. And ask about employee benefits, including paid vacation, health insurance, and paid holidays, which an increasing number of services are offering active employees.□

Q & A

THE SEVERANCE CUSHION

Q: I lost my job, but received a six-month severance package from my employer. I've been under a lot of pressure and would like to take it easy for a month or two. But my friends say I'm foolish if I don't start my job hunt immediately. Are they right?

A: It depends on several factors: your job level, your marketability, and your financial situation. Generally speaking, the higher your job level, the longer it will take to find another position. There are simply fewer such jobs around, and employers often take their time replacing experienced people. If you are confident that your skills and experience are in demand even if the general hiring scene is slow (or you are willing to relocate), you can afford to take a short sabbatical. But that also presumes that you can comfortably cover your financial obligations for at least nine months to a year. No matter how bright you feel your future prospects are, it's a smart idea to immediately begin laying the groundwork for a job search by letting ex-colleagues and friends know that you are looking, by attending meetings or job fairs for professionals in your field, and by researching companies you would like to work for. □

"UNDERCOVER" JOB HUNTING IS IN YOUR BEST INTEREST

Looking for a new job when you are working nine-to-five is not easy, but there are ways to minimize the risk of having your boss learn of your plans. Keeping your job search under wraps is especially important if your relationship with your boss is not great; discovery may give him or her the excuse to let you go. Even if you get along, it's in your best interest to be as discreet as possible. Follow these guidelines to prevent suspicion.

1. Don't share your dissatisfaction with others at work. If you are looking around because your job or your boss is making you unhappy, save your complaints for friends outside the office, family members, or only the most trusted of colleagues.

2. Do resume mailings from home. The risk in working on cover letters or sending out resumes from your desk even if you have the time is that a busybody coworker or your boss may catch you in the act—or you may inadvertently leave evidence of your activity on your desk.

3. Don't include your office number on your resume. Chances are a prospective employer will call you at work if you do. It's far better to give a home phone number and indicate the best hours to reach you. If a family member or friend isn't around during the day (when most employers make their calls), consider investing in an answering machine or paying monthly for a voicemail messaging service (often available through your local phone company) or an answering service.

4. Let interviewers know about your concern for confidentiality. Once you get to the interviewing stage, it doesn't hurt to mention that if your employer learns of it through routine reference checking, your relationship or job might be in jeopardy.

5. Resist the temptation to use the phone at your desk to contact employers. Unless you can close your office door (and do so regularly to concentrate), chances are your conversations will be overheard and correctly interpreted by the astute eavesdropper. It's smarter to schedule a half- or full-day off periodically to make necessary calls, or make them on a break from a nearby pay phone.

6. Don't break your wardrobe pattern. Few clues are more obvious than showing up for work in a suit or clothing that's far dressier than what you normally wear. Unless you can come up with a believable excuse for your appearance, it's better to take a half-day off for an interview or pull a Clark Kent wardrobe switch at your health club or at home.

7. Try not to let your job search or your dissatisfaction affect your work performance. Coming in late, taking long lunch hours, and leaving early are not only tip-offs that you might be job hunting, but taking too much time off can also affect the quality of your work. Even if you find a job quickly, it's best to leave on good terms.

8. Be tight-lipped about any imminent job offers. No matter how confident you feel, say nothing until you have an offer letter in hand and give notice to your boss.□

NEED MORAL SUPPORT AND MOTIVATION? JOIN A JOB CLUB

If you are out of work and need a shot in the arm to keep up your spirits and new ideas on how to find your next position, hook up with a job club. Because they are free or low cost (fees range from $50 to $200 for twenty to thirty hours of counseling), they are a great option if you have to keep a close watch on your cash flow.

How They Can Help

Job clubs can provide a great environment for networking. The more homogeneous the group (that is, the more alike participants' professions, fields, or levels of experience are), the more useful the leads are likely to be.

They are also a great forum for discovering new ways to market your skills and experiences, and to get feedback about how to improve your appearance, speech, or presentation.

Finally, job clubs can help you build up your self-esteem. Friends and relatives may try to help you recover, but there's nothing like being with others who are on the same emotional rollercoaster and facing similar career challenges to help you put the situation in perspective.

How to Choose One

Job clubs meet in places of worship, libraries, community organizations and the offices of career counselors and outplacement firms. You can find them by checking your local paper or church bulletin, or the job information centers of a public library. Another source: the weekly "Calendar of Events" in the *National Business Employment Weekly.*

If you are fortunate enough to live in a metropolitan area, you may have a choice of several groups. The best way to decide if a particular group is likely to work well for you is to visit several and look for these things:

● The size of the group. Ten to twelve people is a good size; it allows everyone a chance to participate.
● Frequency of meetings. Once (or better yet, twice) a week gives a sense of immediacy and continuity.
● Length and structure of meetings. Two to three hours, including time for informal networking, is ideal. Some clubs have an informal agenda, during which time participants bring up problems they have experienced or share

self-assessment exercises or job search techniques they have learned. Other clubs feature talks or presentations on particular topics each week.

● The accountability factor. Some clubs require participants to report on their successes and failures each week and to announce what they intend to do by the next meeting. That's a plus if you find that you're procrastinating about making calls or sending out resumes.

● How skilled the facilitator is. Some come from a sales and marketing background; others are professional career counselors, therapists, or outplacement specialists. More important than their professional qualifications is whether their efforts result in effective meetings and generate an atmosphere of trust and cooperation. If you have misgivings after watching them in action, ask participants who have been there longer for their opinion.

Beware clubs whose facilitators may have a conflict of interest; some free clubs operate as a way for that facilitator to attract paying clients or sell a job-related service.

Finally, keep in mind that to get the most out of a club you have to be prepared to attend on a regular basis and be willing to help your fellow participants. The more willing you are to share advice, experiences, and job leads, the more you'll find others are willing to help you out, too.☐

HEARD ON THE GRAPEVINE: YOUR DAYS ARE NUMBERED

Few office rumors are more unsettling than the one that implies that you may soon be history. If the rumor of your potential demise comes from a credible source, it pays to check things out. It's best to find out from the person who is likely to know best: Your boss. When you do, be prepared to:

1. Talk about it sooner than later. The longer you ruminate about it, the more defensive you may become. Bring up the matter in a matter-of-fact way. You might say: "I heard the craziest thing this morning—that our department is about to be cut in half and that my job is in the 'to cut' column."

2. Hear one of several possible responses. Your boss may say, "That is crazy and it's not true." Or your boss may try to give the impression that all's well, but her tone of voice or body language makes you suspect otherwise. Finally, your boss may confirm that the rumor is true.

3. Ask for an impromptu review. If your boss reassures you that you have nothing to worry about, it's a good time to ask his opinion on what you could be doing better. Why? Because most bosses appreciate employees who invite their feedback on performance issues. It also conveys the impression that you really do care about doing a good job.

4. Take the news in stride. If you learn that your job may be on the line, don't be defensive or adversarial. Instead, find out as much as you can about the future. If the department is facing budget cuts and your boss is considering eliminating your position and others, find out when the decision is likely to be made. It's worth asking whether there is anything you can do to make a case for your boss or senior management to reconsider keeping you on board.

5. Waste no time starting to job hunt if you discover your days are numbered. That does not mean you should neglect your job responsibilities; after all, you may still need a recommendation from your boss. But get the word out to former colleagues and anyone else who may know of a job lead immediately so that you can minimize the time between leaving your job and starting a new one.□

THE POWER OF POSITIVE THINKING

Your first reaction to losing your job may well be: "This cannot be happening to me." Once you get over the shock, you may experience feelings of anger: "How could my employer do this to me after everything I have done for him?" The next stage is to act on the anger in a positive way. Here's how:

1. Hook into a good support system. Tell your family and friends that their support and interest is important to you, and ask them to continue acting as cheerleaders. Another possibility is to start attending a job support group.

2. Keep your job search activity level high. It's the best way for you to feel you are in charge and doing something about changing your situation.

3. Expand your horizons. If you have not already begun considering related jobs and industries in which you can use your skills, do it now. Job hunters who too narrowly define their job target encounter more rejection.

4. Use imagery to keep in a positive mindset. While you are waiting to go into an interview, visualize yourself making a positive impression on the employer, being offered the job, and going to work in your new job. Doing so provides motivation to put in an extra effort to be your best.

5. Question your negative beliefs. Instead of thinking, "I'm no good," tell yourself: "I lost my job, but that does not mean I'm no good." Believing in your self-worth will ward off feelings of depression.□

HELPING SOMEONE YOU LOVE

Sometimes the person who is unemployed and acting depressed does not see his or her own problem. If you are the spouse, parent, or loved one, you can best help by bringing the out-of-character behavior to the person's attention and stating your feelings and your concern.

You might say, for example: "You are watching television six hours a day, not doing household chores, and drinking beer more than you used to. That's annoying to me, but even more important, I'm concerned that you are so unhappy that you are no longer looking for work."

If the person puts you off by saying he or she will try to do better, offer to help make a plan of action, and try to get the person involved in some kind of daily exercise (which increases the sense of control over one's body and one's life).

Don't wait for the signs of deep depression—not shaving or bathing for days, frequently losing one's train of thought, having difficulty doing tasks that used to be simple—to suggest that the person get professional help. Your family doctor or a community health line can often recommend a psychologist or community mental health clinic.□

CHECKLIST

ARE YOU—OR SOMEONE YOU LOVE—DEPRESSED?

Here are the warning signs of depression:

✔ Changes in eating or sleep patterns

✔ Drinking alcoholic beverages or smoking more often than usual (or resuming those habits after having quit)

✔ Feelings of guilt or lowered self-esteem

✔ A loss of sexual urge

✔ Low energy (even after a good night's sleep)□

WHAT TO TELL
THE KIDS

Hiding a job loss and trying to camouflage the resulting financial strain from children can create more problems than it solves. Even preschoolers know that all's not well when a parent who is normally at work spends more time at home, or they hear their parents argue. Here's how to walk the fine line between saying too much—and not enough.

Inform your children about your situation as events unfold. With young children, the explanation might be as simple as, "I'm not going to my old job anymore because I'm looking for a new one." With older children, it's best to start off with a simple statement such as, "I've been laid off because the company is cutting back," and answer whatever questions they have.

Don't put on a happy face for show. It's important to let children know that you are angry, resentful, or depressed about losing your job; the risk of not doing so is that they may feel responsible. And they're more likely to bring up their own fears and emotions with you.

Explain the possible financial implications of your job loss. If you know you will not be able to afford things your children have come to expect, tell them so. Rather than make the decision about what your children will have to do without, it's better to ask for their input on how they can save money. Even if their ideas are not viable (be sure to explain why), they are likely to feel less disappointed because they were consulted. Realize, too, that unless your children perceive that you are making sacrifices, they will resent the sacrifices imposed on them.

Tell your children what your job loss will mean for each of them beyond money matters. If you need privacy to make phone calls to potential employers, say that's why they must not bother you or must play outside. If the family car is less available for their use because of your changed schedule, explain that before you "ruin" their fun.

Be receptive to your children's offers to help. If your child is old enough to take on a small money-making responsibility and wants to do so, be supportive so long as the work does not interfere with her studies or other activities important to her.

Be reassuring. With the bad news you dole out should come a message of hope for the future. Talk about your plans to find a job. Mention the experiences of other parents the children know who have successfully been through this kind of situation. And, most important, let your children know that you love them and want to do everything you can to keep them happy.□

WHEN A SPOUSE IS FIRED

DO make your first response one of total, unconditional empathy.

DO encourage him to talk about his feelings or plans once the shock of losing his job subsides.

DON'T impose your help without asking first. If your partner says she wants your help, you can critique her resume, network for her, or clip help wanted ads and job leads from business articles in the newspaper. But remember that some people prefer empathy rather than problem-solving help.

DO realize that your partner may change his mind, even if he initially encouraged your input. Be sensitive to his verbal and non-verbal reactions to your advice and help.

DON'T be too blunt if you think that your partner's appearance, presentation skills, or attitude may be hurting her interview or job chances. Instead of offering your advice on how to improve any of these factors, suggest she get advice from a business colleague or friend whose opinion she respects or from an expert—a speech coach or image consultant, for example.

DON'T express your resentment about your partner's job loss to him. Justified or not, you will probably begin to experience some resentment once it begins to have an impact on your finances or emotional health. Share how you feel with a friend, who can help you put your feelings in perspective.

DO get help if your relationship is on the rocks. Even the best of relationships is likely to be jarred by a job loss. If the period of unemployment or financial strain is prolonged, expect major relationship tremors. Short-term counseling with a professional marriage counselor or through your place of worship or a community health center is a good idea.□

CREATE A PORTFOLIO

Savvy job hunters make an effort to distinguish themselves from the competition by showing prospective employers examples of their work or results of their efforts whenever possible. The employers you interview with may not be expecting such a portfolio, but are likely to be impressed if you put one together with thought and care.

What should a portfolio contain? If your work is visual— graphic design, desktop publishing, illustration—you should feature samples of your work. But if the results of your work are less tangible, include items that show the results of your efforts, for example, a program of an event you planned, a direct marketing piece that features your ideas, or letters from satisfied customers.

Select the most representative pieces and arrange them in a way that they can be easily understood. Include a brief typed description of what the item is so that the reader can easily grasp its context. A letter of appreciation or commendation from your boss or management would be terrific to include.□

WHAT TO ASK FOR WHEN YOU'RE REORGANIZED OUT OF A JOB

During a reorganization, merger, or downsizing, employers are often willing to help out employees they are letting go. If help isn't offered, ask your boss or someone in management with whom you are on good terms for the following:

✔ Severance pay. Ask your boss to go to bat for you and get as much as she can.

✔ Outplacement assistance. A range of services from job counseling to financial advisory help is available. Your boss may be able to persuade management to pay for the services you feel would be most beneficial.

✔ Use of office facilities. Ask if you can continue coming into the office (not necessarily your current quarters) to use the telephone, computer and copying services until you find a new position.

✔ Help with job leads. This may be the best request of all because it's something over which your boss has total control and may be the quickest way to find a new position. Find out if he's willing to make introductory phone calls on your behalf.□

CHAPTER 2

RESUMES AND COVER LETTERS

COVER LETTER BLOOPERS CAN HURT YOU

Sending a cover letter with your resume is a bit of an insurance policy; if it's thoughtful and well-written, it can increase the time a prospective employer spends reading your resume. But be sure to avoid these mistakes:

THE "TO WHOM IT MAY CONCERN" GREETING

If you make the effort to direct your letter to a specific person, it's more likely to be read. Why? Because you have taken the time to investigate who will be screening resumes. A phone call to the employer is usually all that is required to get the correct spelling and title of the person. The exception: help wanted ads that list only a post office box. In that case, it's best to use the gender-blind greeting, "Dear Employer."

COOKIE-CUTTER CLAUSES

Your cover letter is more likely to catch the attention and interest of an employer if you avoid over-used phrases. Letters that open with the words, "Enclosed is my resume," show no imagination. Other trite phrases to avoid include: "As you will see from my resume...," and "I have heard great things about you (or your department or company)."

It's much better to begin with a more lively thought, such as: "Perhaps we're the answer to each other's prayers," or "If I had to write a description of my dream job, it would have been the copy that appeared in your help wanted ad." A bit of exaggeration in the interest of drama will not hurt unless you're applying for a job in a traditionally conservative field, such as banking or insurance. Even then, a spark of creativity sometimes catches the fancy of the person screening resumes.

THE STORY OF MY LIFE SYNDROME

Going into too much detail about who you are and why you are qualified for the job in a cover letter will not win you extra points. In fact, a long letter makes it harder for the reader to quickly determine why he should take a serious look at your resume.

Here's what essential to communicate: who you are (a recent graduate, an accountant with five years' experience); what job you are applying for (employers are often trying to fill more than one position at a time and need to separate resumes into appropriate piles); and one or two facts about your skills and experience that particularly qualify you for the job.

ME, ME, ME

It's fine to mention several reasons why an employer might find your background of interest. But if you fail to point out how you could help solve a problem or accomplish something on a hiring manager's or company's wishlist, your letter and resume may get only a glance. It's far better to be seen as an applicant who understands the employer's needs, not someone who is simply looking to better his or her own situation. Before you can make this kind of statement, however, you do your homework, either by talking to employees you know at that company or by reviewing print information, products, or services. Once you identify a problem or goal, you can link it to your own skills and experiences. For example: "I'm confident that I can use my programming and graphic design skills to help you create multimedia promotions that would give your sales force an edge over the competition."

DOLLAR SIGNS

There's nothing to be gained and much to lose by mentioning your current salary or what your financial expectations for your next position are. If either is beyond what an employer thinks she wants to pay, you may never have the opportunity to convince her in person that you're worth more. If you have been underpaid or ask for less than the going rate, you may get an interview and even an offer but at a salary that's not competitive.

MISSPELLINGS AND TYPOS

If you are applying for a job that requires attention to detail, one of these can kill your chances for consideration. If you are creating a cover letter on a computer with a spell-check feature, use it. If not, look up any words you are not sure of and proofread the letter several times. Having a friend or relative read it over for mistakes is advisable, too.

THE SICK TYPEWRITER BLUES

If you don't have access to a state-of-the art electric typewriter or a computer, have a typing service or copy shop produce your cover letter for you. Make sure it's set up like a business letter, with proper placement of the inside address and date; consistent indentations; space between paragraphs; and with the body of the letter centered. You want to create the impression that you are the perfect candidate; the first test of that is a perfect cover letter.□

STOP STALLING: REVISE YOUR RESUME NOW

Few job hunting tools are more critical than a well-conceived resume. It's often the first basis on which an employer forms an impression of you; and the amount of thought that goes into the content and presentation often makes the difference of whether or not you are called for an interview.

Revising a resume is, however, not unlike scheduling a dental checkup; most people put it off for as long as they can. The task of creating and editing text may seem formidable, but you can make both more manageable and your resume stronger if you do the following things:

● **Get outside opinions.** Ask one or more friends or colleagues whose judgment you trust to critique your current resume. Encourage them do so with pen in hand. Tell them you are interested in their citing wording that is unclear, descriptions that are lackluster, or information they feel is extraneous.

● **Target problem areas.** Review what your critics have to say and change easily correctable problems. Then judge for yourself whether your current resume is guilty of a major sin of omission: Too few or no descriptions of your accomplishments. Save the task of listing your successes— small and big—for the next step.

● **Quantify results whenever possible.** Numbers can paint a picture far more effectively than words and can give the person reading the resume a better context for evaluating your responsibilities and accomplishments.

● **Ask someone to play the role of interviewer.** Having someone ask you questions about what you did on the job and the results you got can help you get information down on paper more quickly than if you try to go it alone. The two of you should focus your efforts on those jobs you or your critics have identified as being the most obvious candidates for improvement.

● **Take notes.** Either you or your interviewer should be taking notes during your interview. Or turn on a tape recorder so that you can easily retrieve the words and phrases you used or that your interviewer suggested.

● **Incorporate new information and wording to create your new resume.** If you feel you have the grace of an elephant walking a tightrope when you put pen to paper, use this simple resume phraseology: (1) an action verb + (2) object or people + (3) to or for whom; of, on, or from what; by, through, or with what. Example: (1) Conducted (2) preadmissions evaluations (3) of substance abusers. You can, of course, add more clauses to make the description even more specific.

● **Add examples and information to your job descriptions that show that you are a saver** (someone who knows how to save time, effort or money); an initiator (someone who is creative and not afraid to take risks); a good people person; a "can do" type; and an effective communicator (someone with a good command of the English language and the ability to speak with bosses, colleagues, and customers).

● **Finally, make sure your resume design says "read me."** Unless you have a computer and feel comfortable experimenting with white space, placement of headings, and other graphic elements to test for the best look, have a copy shop with desktop publishing services design your resume.☐

RESUME DESIGN

The best way to make sure your resume gets read is to make it visually appealing.

DO make sure there is plenty of white space. Make your margins at least one-inch (top, bottom, left, and right) and add an extra space or half-space around headings.

DON'T select a typeface that's ornate or unusual. It may be difficult to read and fail to convey what you hope—that you're not just a run-of-the-mill candidate.

DO use a typeface that's clean and professional looking; best bets are Helvetica, Palatino, Times, and New York.

DON'T use different typefaces within your resume. If you want to make a title or group of words stand out, use italics, boldface, underlining, or a different size of the same typeface.

DON'T choose a typeface that's so small it's hard to read. It's better to choose space-efficient typeface rather than a smaller point size of a typeface that fits fewer characters on a line. Times is the most type-efficient typeface that can be found on most word-processing programs.

DON'T use dingbats, that is, symbols such as thumbs up or down, arrows or exclamation points. Stick to bullets (the option key + 8 on Microsoft Word), dashes, or simple indents to separate text.

DO be consistent in your use of graphic elements and capitalization. If, for example, you have chosen to underline job titles, make sure all of them are underlined.

DON'T type your resume. Too many job hunters have access to word processing and desktop publishing programs that are capable of producing resumes that make their typewriter counterparts look like poor cousins. So consider the $30 to $40 you will spend for a copy center to keyboard in your text an investment in your next job.

DON'T use a pastel or unusual paper for your resume. A conventional white or off-white, light beige, or gray paper that is a 20-pound bond or 50-pound offset is best.

DO have your resume reproduced professionally. The high-quality professional copiers used in copy shops or a laser printer (particularly good if you plan to customize your resume to particular employers) are two good choices.□

DON'T GIVE SHORT SHRIFT TO ORDINARY JOBS

Most people—even company presidents—have held ordinary jobs at some point in their life. Work experience, whether you got it as a lifeguard, as a fast-food cook, or as a camp counselor, can help you land an interview and a job. Including them on your resume is very important because it shows that you know how to get along with others, can take direction, and complete tasks.

The mistake that many resume writers make is assuming that the reader knows what job tasks their ordinary job involved or minimizing the experience by failing to describe the extent of their responsibilities or accomplishments.

The way to avoid that mistake is to use descriptive language and include details that make your job sound important. If, for example, you worked as a camp counselor, you might list the following points under your job title and dates of employment: (1) Supervised craft and recreational activities of ten nine year olds eight hours a day; (2) Provided swimming instruction to over 100 beginners over the course of the summer; (3) Solved crises—big and small—of my charges, including a water rescue effort for which I received commendation from the camp director.

Information that conveys the message that you're motivated, responsible, and hardworking sends an important message to a prospective employer, no matter how different the job you're applying for is.□

AVOID THESE RESUME EXCESSES

A resume should give prospective employers a good idea of who you are, but you need not reveal every wrinkle and blemish. Including any of the following personal information may hurt you more than help you—or, at the very least, be extraneous.

- Your age or date of birth
- Your marital status
- The names or ages of your children
- Your spouse's occupation
- Whether you own or rent your home
- Details of your military service record (unless applying to a firm that values military experience)
- Type of car you own
- Your health status
- Your salary requirements
- Political or religious affiliations□

REDUCE EDUCATION RESUME INFORMATION?

Q: I have ten years of job experience and am updating my resume. Should I eliminate the big projects and extracurricular activities I was involved in in college?

A: Once you're out of school for five years or more, list only the names of your degrees, the colleges that awarded them and when, and whether you graduated with honors or distinction. Co-op jobs or important internships you participated in as a college student can be listed under "Work Experience." If you think the project you worked on or organization you participated in would be of particular interest to an employer, you can always mention it in a cover letter or interview.□

USE AN INTERVIEWER'S FIRST NAME?

Q: I'm writing a follow-up letter to an interviewer who called me by my first name during the interview. Everyone in the office called him by his first name. Should I write, "Dear Dave" or "Dear Mr. Smith" in my letter?

A: Unless he specifically said, "Just call me Dave," you're better off addressing him by his surname. You don't want to risk offending him by presuming that it's fine to call him by his first name. And addressing a person by their last name is a sign of respect, which only helps when you're job hunting.□

RESUME TRIMMING TECHNIQUES

You can save valuable space for more important information by deleting the following words or headings:

IDEA

SMART

- Resume of
- Responsible for
- Position or Job Title
- References Available On Request

Beyond that, you can:

- Abbreviate or eliminate descriptions of responsibilities for positions you held years ago or that are not relevant to the position you are now seeking.
- Eliminate any personal information other than name, address, and phone number.
- Don't bother including the line "References available on request" (you can always provide names and numbers on a separate sheet with contact information).
- Substitute an action verb for the words "responsible for."□

HOW TO EXPLAIN WORK GAPS

You're not alone if you did not work for a period of months or years during your career. Whether the time off was your choice or not, it's important to let prospective employers know why your career was interrupted. The danger of not explaining a gap that lasted more than a few months is that a prospective employer may rule you out if there are a number of other similarly qualified applicants for a position whose resumes don't raise questions.

Here are three work gap scenarios and how to explain them:

UNEMPLOYMENT OF MORE THAN SEVERAL MONTHS

It's probably best to acknowledge in a cover letter that you have been looking, and succinctly state why you feel your efforts were unsuccessful, without blaming anyone. You might say, for example, that you limited your search to a specific type of position, company, or geographic area. Make it clear why you are widening your search. It might be because you have taken courses that have added to your skills or knowledge. Or that through career counseling or networking, you have confirmed that your skills are transferable to other industries. Another scenario: If you have only recently begun your job search because you needed the time to carefully consider your next move, say so.

TIME OUT TO RAISE A FAMILY

If you have been away from the work force for years because you were raising a family, you can simply write: 1988–1992 — Took time off to care full time for my children. It wouldn't hurt to mention in your cover letter how you kept in touch with trends and changes in your field or how you applied your professional skills in other contexts. If you left a job in corporate communications, for example, explain that you produced the monthly eight-page school newsletter for a year. If your job involved raising money, mention your role as a school auction chair and the proceeds realized from the auction.

PERSONAL HEALTH PROBLEMS

If an accident or serious illness forced you to take time off, mention it in a cover letter provided you are completely recovered and your illness is not likely to recur. Stress your ability (or doctor's approval) to get back to work. If, however, your current health status is limiting in some way (either because of the possible bias of a potential employer, or because you need accommodation to do the job, for example, a desk chair that enable you to sit for long periods of time), don't bring up the reason for your time away until you're in the job interview.□

INCLUDE REASONS FOR LEAVING ON RESUME?

Q: Should you include reasons for leaving various jobs on your resume?

A: Usually it's better to wait until a face-to-face interview to talk about why you parted company with employers you have worked for. Most departures cannot adequately be explained in a few words or even a sentence or two; you may hurt your chances of getting an interview because your explanation raises more questions than it answers. It's particularly important to impress an employer with your experience, skills, and ability to work with others if you were let go. Even if your dismissal was unrelated to your job performance, you will boost your chances of getting hired if the interviewer has a chance to see and talk to you about other issues first.

The only time that including your reasons for leaving on a resume can help is if these three conditions exist: (1) Many candidates are competing for a job; (2) Resume screening is likely to be substantial; and (3) Your reasons for leaving are positive, that is, you left to accept a more challenging or better-paying position.

The best place to include your reasons for leaving is in a line just below the descriptions of your responsibilities and accomplishments on a particular job.□

HOW TO PROMOTE YOUR ATHLETIC SKILLS

Q: I'm a good athlete. Some of the companies I'm applying to have organized teams and leagues that take their games very seriously. I've heard that job applicants with sports abilities sometimes have an edge over those who don't. I'd like to make interviewers aware of my sports skills, but how do I slip that into conversation naturally?

A: One way to tip off prospective employers that you are an avid athlete even before they meet you is to mention your skills or experience in appropriate sections of the resume. If you're a fairly recent graduate, you might incorporate your participation in a sport into an "Extracurricular Activities" section. If you're not, you can always mention sports under your "Interests" section. Instead of just listing the sport, briefly describe your accomplishments or involvement. If you were captain of your college tennis team and had a great season record, say so.

In the interview, don't hesitate to bring up the subject after the job responsibilities and other important issues have been discussed. Say that you've heard there is a baseball team, and ask if company newcomers are welcome to participate. The interviewer's reaction will tell you whether your sports ability is an asset.□

WHAT QUESTIONS TO ASK A RESUME PREPARATION SERVICE?

If writing a resume and sending out cover letters is a job you would rather pay someone to help you with than do yourself, be sure that your money is well spent by asking these questions:

● How long has the company been in business?

● What are the credentials of the person creating or revising your resume?

● Can you pay for individual services such as resume creation a la carte or must you pay for a package of services?

● What is the breakdown of costs for each service and what does each include?

● How long does the consultation for the resume creation/revision last?

● How will the person preparing your resume get the information that will be featured in it (e.g., by having you fill in a form, asking you questions)?

● Has the person preparing your resume ever worked with someone at your job level or in your field before?

● Does the service provide both hard copies (how many) and a diskette (which software program and version) of your resume and cover letters?

● How does the service identify employers who will receive your resume?

● What kinds of results have other clients obtained from cover letter and resume mailings sent out by the service?□

WHERE RESUME GIMMICKS GET YOU?

Have your resume delivered along with a lunchtime pizza to the personnel department? Tuck it into a bouquet for the company president? Or perhaps attach it to a box of chocolates? That's sure to get it noticed, right?

Yes, but unless your gimmick is carefully conceived and targeted to appeal to the sensibility or sense of humor of the person receiving it, it could backfire.

If the president of the company happens to be a connoisseur of fine chocolates, sending less than the best may result in your being seen as someone with poor taste or judgment.

If, on the other hand, you have read up on the company and discovered that the president is a model train enthusiast, it would not be out of line to enclose a recent article on the topic or a notice about an upcoming model train convention with your resume and a cover letter. In short: A personal gesture that shows your ingenuity or creativity is far more likely to get noticed and perhaps result in an interview than is a gimmick.□

WHITE LIES DON'T PAY

It can be tempting, oh so tempting, to inflate, exaggerate, or be otherwise "creative" in constructing the details on your resume. A slight distortion of the truth can make a job seem more important than it really was, put you in the running for a job because you earned a particular academic credential or license, or make your accomplishments come across a little grander. Such a misrepresentation may increase your chances of getting a call for an interview. or a job offer. Don't succumb.

Why? Because it's too easy to get caught. Employers often do thorough reference checks. If they find an inconsistency, your candidacy will probably be in jeopardy. You may be given a chance to explain—or you may simply be put in the reject pile.

Here's what employers can easily verify:

JOB TITLE, DATES OF EMPLOYMENT, AND SALARY INFORMATION. These

are the bare-bone facts that even the most wary employers will provide. But some will answer questions about your job responsibilities, your performance, and promotions or demotions. A few may comment on your mental stability, and any alcohol, drug, health, or family problems that interfered with your performance even when it's illegal to do so.

ACADEMIC RECORDS. Schools and universities will confirm whether an applicant has attended their institution, the dates of attendance and graduation, and the name of the degree or certificate earned.

CREDIT HISTORY. Credit bureau reports not only list the balances on your bank accounts, loans, and credit cards, but any late payments or judgments against you as a result of nonpayment.

CRIMINAL RECORD. Any crime of which you have been found guilty—from drunk driving to shoplifting to substance abuse—can be found in public records and is accessible to anyone who cares to look for them.

White lies should not be confused with putting your best foot forward. If your contributions to a successful project were significant, it's fine to choose words that reflect that. Similarly, if a change was introduced because of your efforts or ideas, don't hesitate to take credit for it. But don't overstate the case. If what you really did was to help the person who made something big happen, don't choose words that give the impression that you were instrumental in making it happen. Savvy employers are skilled at discerning whether what you claim as a success was likely given your background, job title, and responsibilities. Use the words "assisted, contributed, acted as a member of a team who..." in describing an achievement in an interview or on your resume to avoid the problem.

The bottom line: Toot your horn but don't blow it.□

 DO'S & DON'TS

JOB OBJECTIVE

To include a job objective on your resume...or not? That is a hotly debated topic. Some resume experts say that a job objective belongs in a cover letter; employers claim that a job objective at the top of a resume is a useful screening device. If you decide to use one, follow these guidelines:

DO make sure your objective is supported by your experience and skills. The biggest sin: Aiming too high when your credentials and competition for jobs doesn't warrant such a grandiose ambition.

DON'T include several job objectives in one resume. Instead, develop separate resumes, each of which is tailored to support a particular objective.

DO be as specific as possible. If you know the title of the job you hope to get, use it. If you are not sure which staff positions are open within the department you want to work for, it's fine to say that you would like a job in a particular department where you could best contribute your (name one or two) skills or experience.

DON'T be too wordy. It's fine to include words that say which skills or experience you'd like to use in a position or career area, but keep it short and sweet.☐

DELIVER THE LETTER (AND RESUME), THE SOONER, THE BETTER?

Fewer actions are more satisfying than sending off a resume and cover letter when you hear of an interesting job opening. But will you get a leg up on the competition by faxing your resume?

Probably not—unless the employer has made it clear in the help wanted ad or through the person you heard about the opening from that faxing is fine. Getting a resume on fax rather than bond paper is like getting a birthday present in its store bag rather than wrapping paper: It's not nearly as visually appealing. If you want your resume to be among the first that is received, it's better to have it hand delivered or sent via an overnight mail delivery service, both of which are more likely to be handed to or put on the desk of the person you want to see it.☐

LINE UP YOUR REFERENCES IN ADVANCE

Most job hunters give little thought to the last line they often tack on their resume: References Available on Request. But since employers often do touch base with previous employers or those who know your work habits, it's smart to ask potential references if you can give their names to prospective employers.

Prepare your list of references as a separate sheet. At the top of the sheet, put your name, address, and phone just as you had it at the top of your resume. Then center the heading, "List of References." Include the following information for each reference you list: the person's name, job title, phone number, name and address of his or her current company, and in what capacity the reference knows you. Here's an example:

Karen Janes, Vice President
Online Services
USA Networking, Inc.
888 Pascal Drive
Menlo Park, California 94025
My immediate supervisor at
USA Networking, 1992-94

The best time to give an employer this reference sheet is at an interview. Be sure to call your references as soon after the interview as you can to alert them that they may be getting a call. Brief them on the company and job you are seeking. You can help them help you by clueing them in about which aspects of your experience, work habits, or qualities you feel are most worth emphasizing.□

Q & A

PROVIDE SALARY HISTORY?

Q: When a help-wanted ad requests that you send your salary history, will you be discounted by the employer if you do not?

A: Not necessarily. Almost 80 percent of human resource executives reported that they would place a phone call to an applicant whose resume interested them, even if the person did not follow an advertisement's salary guidelines, according to a survey conducted by Fox-Morris Associates, a full-service executive search and outplacement consulting firm.

If you fear that your current salary would rule you out as a candidate, explain your salary history in your cover letter. If you are willing to take less for the right job, say so. If you are living in an area of the country where living expenses (and salaries) are high, say that you would be prepared to take a cut that's in line with living expenses in the area in which the employer is located.□

SHOULD JOBS RECEIVE EQUAL WEIGHT ON RESUME?

Q: I have 15 years of experience working for three different employers. Should I give each one equal weight on my resume?

A: No. Many employers and recruiters say that what interests them most is what you have done most recently. It's particularly important to devote more space to your current or most recent position if you work in a field in which technology or new advances mean that you are a "state-of-the-art" type candidate.

Another consideration is which past positions best support your bid for a new position. If your current or most immediate past job is not a likely stepping stone to what you want to do next, it makes sense to spend more time describing earlier jobs. It's smart, however, to explain on your resume or in a cover letter why you took your current or most recent job, what you did on it that would be helpful in the position you are applying for or why you want to get back into the kind of work you had done before. The bottom line is that the employer evaluating your resume will want to see evidence that you have built on your experiences in a way that's understandable and applicable to his or her business.□

INCLUDE PERSONAL INTERESTS ON RESUME

Are you a fan of cyberspace mysteries? Do you collect antique photographs? Are you a triathlete? It's worthwhile to list what you do in your free time as the last item on your resume for two reasons.

1. Interviewers often use this information as a conversational ice breaker in an interview. They know that you will probably feel more comfortable talking about playing ice hockey or doing floral arrangements than you will your qualifications for the job.

2. A prospective employer may share your passion for a sport, hobby, or special interest. And that can help position you as a leading candidate, provided, of course, that you have the right qualifications and experience for the job.

A word of caution: do not include interests that you have no serious involvement with.□

SUCCESS STRATEGIES

REACH A WIDER EMPLOYER AUDIENCE THROUGH A COMPUTER DATABASE

You can get your resume in front of employers you might not otherwise have thought of by registering with a company that operates a resume database. Most services charge a $15 to $50 registration fee. The information on your resume (or a form they provide you to fill out) is then entered into their database. Employer clients search these databases using keyword credentials (e.g., a certain type of degree, years of experience, particular skills) to locate candidates who might fit a position they're trying to fill.

The biggest disadvantage if you are currently employed is the possibility that your resume may be seen by your employer (or clients who may tip off your employer). If you want to protect your identity, ask what privacy safeguards the service offers. The best protection is a service that checks with you before you before releasing your identity and phone number.

Another alternative: the Online Career Center, a non-profit resume and job listing database on the Internet. If you have access, there's no charge to post your resume. If not, you can have a service post it for you for $10. (Mail your full-text resume and a check to: Online Resume Service, 1713 Hemlock Lane, Plainfield, Indiana 46168.) In addition to the job postings from the 140+ member companies who support Online Career Center, job openings from over 3,000 companies who post openings to newsgroups on the Internet are also featured.□

CREATE MORE THAN ONE VERSION OF YOUR RESUME

If you plan to apply for more than one kind of job or for jobs in different types of businesses, you will want to emphasize different aspects of your experience, create more than one version of your resume. Say, for example, that you have had experience as a restaurant hostess and as a hotel front-desk clerk. If you were applying for a job with a restaurant, you would want to dedicate more space to your hostess skills and vice versa. If you have access to a computer, you might even want to consider changing your "boilerplate" resume to suit each position you apply for.□

THE WRITE STUFF: WAYS TO MAKE SURE YOUR LETTER GETS NOTICED

When you write directly to employers about the possibility of setting up a job interview, it's important to do several things to increase the chances of your letter getting noticed.

1. Write to a person who heads up the department you hope to work for. Most human resources and personnel departments are inundated with resumes; yours may get more attention if it goes to a hiring manager. Be sure to check with the company to verify that the person still holds that position.

2. Identify employers whose businesses are in growth industries. This may require your cross-checking information from a directory with current information in business or trade publications. These companies often need people yesterday and are more likely to save and respond to resumes from qualified applicants.

3. Address the question of what you can do for the company in an accompanying cover letter. The more you know about an employer and its products or services, the more specific you can be about what you can offer. At the very least, you can talk about the personal qualities you bring to the job: your willingness to work hard, your ability to cut costs, or your punctuality.

4. Follow up. Your resume and cover letter may get put aside, misfiled, or even lie unopened. A call to the person you wrote to approximately a week after the resume arrives is a must. Ask if he or she received it and whether an interview can be arranged. Be persistent; if you do not get a "yes" right away, call back.□

DID YOU KNOW...

USING THE WRONG SALUTATION CAN TURN OFF AN EMPLOYER?

The biggest cover letter sin you can commit is using "Dear Sir" when you do not know the name of the person who will be reading your resume. To presume that a man will be reviewing it is off-putting to women human resources professionals and managers. Even "Dear Sir or Madam" is a bit stuffy. Avoid the impersonal sounding "To Whom It May Concern." You cannot go wrong with "Dear Personnel Director," or "Dear Prospective Employer."□

CHAPTER 3

JOB SEARCH STRATEGIES

THE RIGHT WAY TO ASK CONTACTS FOR HELP

If you are the kind of person who doesn't feel comfortable asking people for help, particularly if you don't know them well or have never had occasion to do something nice for them, you are not alone. Few job hunters feel at ease calling up colleagues, ex-colleagues, friends, and friends of friends to ask for help. On the other hand, most people do not mind a friendly, polite call asking for their advice—even from someone they have never met. The more such calls you make, the less awkward you will feel.

The more people you connect with, the better your chances of identifying job openings and getting an offer. A contact need not be someone who has the power to hire you. A contact can also be a person who can give you advice, information, or the names of other people who can help you. Just keep the following rules of thumb in mind:

DO ask the person who gives you a contact's name how he or she might be able to help, so that you are better able to make your request.

DO clearly identify yourself when you write or call a contact. Say who suggested you call or how you got the person's name.

DO rehearse your request. It helps to write a script in which you introduce yourself, say who suggested you call, and ask if the person has a few minutes now, or at a more convenient time, to talk to you. Try to limit your description of your experience and what you are looking for to a few concise sentences. Then make your request: Say that you want to discuss what your next step should be, job search strategies, opportunities in that person's field or industry, or job openings in that person's company.

DON'T ask for too much too soon. For example, asking the contact to arrange an interview for you with a department manager before he or she has seen your resume or talked to you personally is overreaching. It's far better to ask the person's advice about whether you have the right qualifications for the position you are seeking (if he is in a position to make such a judgment) or to ask the best way to go about setting up an interview at the company.

DON'T be unprepared when you arrive for a face-to-face meeting. Be ready to ask questions that you feel the person is in a good position to answer. Listen, take notes, and ask follow-up questions. Most people will be flattered that you value their opinion.

DO ask for more leads. If the contact does not know of job openings, ask if he or she can suggest other people you can talk to. If you have made a good impression, chances are good you will come away with more names.

DON'T overstay your welcome. If you have asked for twenty minutes' of a person's time, take the initiative and point out that your time is up. If your contact has the time and inclination, he or she will say, "Don't worry, I have a few more minutes." If he doesn't, ask your last question and graciously make your exit.

DON'T forget to send a thank-you note and keep the person posted on your job progress.

DON'T be discouraged if you do not get a good reception from each person you call. Some people will be more helpful than others.□

WHEN A HEADHUNTER CALLS

Q: I recently got a call from a head-hunter. How do headhunters operate, and is it worth it to return the call?

A: Recruiters, or search consultants, as they prefer to be called, conduct exclusive searches for client companies who pay them to find qualified, experienced candidates to fill a particular position.

Generally speaking, you have nothing to lose (but a little time) and potentially much to gain (a new and better job) by talking to a reputable recruiter. When you do, find out how long the firm has been in business, what type of clients or industries it serves, and how many successful searches it has conducted in the last year. You can also ask whether the firm is a member of a professional association such as the Association of Executive Search Consultants. Members must have been in business for a period of time, meet professional requirements, and agree to adhere to a code of ethics.

Ask the same questions about the position that you would if you were talking to an employer, among them: the job title and responsibilities, who you would be reporting to, the size of the company or division, and the salary and benefits package. Find out, too, what kind of skills and credentials the employer is looking for in candidates.

If the job does not interest you, the recruiter may ask you for recommendations of others to contact. If you're impressed with the recruiter, it's smart to recommend a friend, colleague, or ex-colleague who you think has the right background. That person may be thrilled to hear about the position (particularly if he or she is out of work) and regardless of the outcome, will remember the gesture the next time you have a favor or request. And the recruiter will be inclined to think of you again when doing a new search.□

BE PERSISTENT, BUT NOT OBNOXIOUS

If you really want a job interview with a particular employer, you may have to call a number of times to get it. Why? Because most employers eventually do respond to job hunters who make it known that they really want to work for that company. When making your call, keep these things in mind:

DO sound upbeat and confident. It's important not to let on that you are upset that your calls have not been returned.

DO leave a polite and straightforward message with the person answering the phone if you cannot get through to the person you hoped to reach. You might say, for example: "I was calling to find out if Mr. Smythe has begun arranging interviews or if any new job openings have come up and to let you know of my continued interest in the company."

DON'T make a pest of yourself. How often you get in touch with an employer depends on the circumstances. If you know there is a job opening, calling every three days is fine. If you are trying to set up an interview but do not know if an opening exists, calling every week is probably more appropriate.

DON'T bungle the conversation once you do get through. Rehearse what you want to say in advance so that you come across as an intelligent candidate.

So long as you are politely persistent, the worst thing that can happen is that you will be told, "We aren't interested." □

SHOULD THIS GRADUATE NARROWCAST JOB SEARCH?

Q: I will be graduating from college this spring (laden with student loan obligations) and hope to line up a job before graduation through on-campus recruiting. The problem is that most of the type of employers I would like to work for are not visiting my campus. I did go on an interview, which led to an on-site interview and a job offer with an employer in an industry I had not considered. Should I play it safe and accept it or try my luck at landing a job in the field I really want to be in?

A: You owe it to yourself to look for a job in your top-choice field. Why? Because you will never know what could have been until you do. If you sidetrack your career dreams at this early point, you may find it difficult to pursue them later without taking a cut in pay.

Just because recruiters from your field are absent from your campus does not mean there are no jobs available. And you need not wait until you graduate to start your search. Use the resources of your career planning and placement office to identify potential employers. Ask for the names of alumni who are working in the field—they are worth contacting for information and guidance. Attend resume and cover letter writing workshops to make sure yours is the best it can be. You can start contacting employers now provided you have the time to follow up with phone calls and can schedule interviews.

You need not turn down the one job offer you got cold. Just say that you do not feel ready to make a decision yet because you are exploring other options. Leave the door open by asking whether you can get back in touch with the employer after graduation. □

51
●

SCOUT OUT OPENINGS WITH SMALL BUSINESSES

Large or well-known companies are often inundated with resumes because job hunters do not know of or seek out positions that may be available with small employers. However, many new jobs are created by businesses employing 100 or fewer employees, which is why it is to your advantage to scout out such openings. Here's how to successfully pitch yourself as a job candidate to a small employer.

1. Identify and contact employers you would like to work for. Small employers often rely on word-of-mouth referrals to replace departing employees because they do not have the time to conduct elaborate candidate searches. So if you make yourself known to an employer by sending a resume and cover letter and following up by phone, you create the possibility of getting contacted when a position opens up. It's smart to ask for an interview even if an opening does not currently exist; the employer is more likely to remember you if he or she has met you face-to-face.

Be persistent but polite in your attempts to contact the office manager or president—that person may be hard to get on the phone, but that does not mean that he or she is not interested in talking to you. It's in your best interest to develop a friendly rapport with the person who answers the phone. At small organizations, the gatekeeper often has access to the top people and can put in a good word for you if you treat him or her with respect.

2. Be open to personal questions. While small employers need competent people, they are more likely to try to determine if they feel comfortable with you—an important factor in a closely knit working environment. So they may ask more questions about your personal life and interests (even some questions that are, technically speaking, illegal) than they do about your skills and experience. If you like the person and the company, it's in your best interest to be forthcoming.

3. Emphasize your flexibility. Job descriptions at small firms are not written in stone; in fact, most employees wear a number of hats. Talk about your willingness to pitch in to do whatever is needed and your ability to learn skills or integrate information that is outside your area of expertise. Cite examples of both: the time when you helped your secretary and staff collate and staple reports that needed to get out, or how you taught yourself word processing so that you could type your own first drafts on the computer.

The flip side of emphasizing your flexi

bility is to ask specific questions to determine just what it is you are expected to do so that you have no illusions about how you will be spending your work day.

4. Ask questions about the company's business and track record. Small organizations do not expect you to know this information in advance, but employers are likely to be impressed if you care enough to ask because of their intense, personal involvement with their business. You might ask for a description of its products or services; what the company's history of sales, profits, and employee growth has been for the last three years; and what its goals and direction are. And, of course, be sure to ask why the job is available—because the employee was promoted or left the company or whether it is a newly created position.

The employer's answers can give you a basis for judging how stable and profitable the business is, and whether it is the kind of place where you can grow and advance personally.

5. Be prepared for an on-the-spot job offer. If you are being interviewed by one of the top people in the com-pany, you may well be asked if you want the job before the interview ends. You will not necessarily lose out on the opportunity if you do not jump at the prospect, but be sure to convey your interest and ask if you can get back to the person in a day or two.□

HELP WANTED ADS: HOW TO READ BETWEEN THE LINES

It's not enough to circle help wanted ads that match the kind of job you hope to find. Hidden in the fine print of the classifieds are dozens of other job leads. Here's what to look for beyond the obvious jobs:

Positions for which you're under- or overqualified

The ad may say "five years of experience required," but if the job sounds enticing, you should respond whether you have three or seven years of experience. Why? If you have less than the desired experience, the employer may be willing to consider you anyway, given your knowledge of the industry, special skills, or willingness to be trained for what you don't know. Or the employer may be interested in hiring someone into a junior position once the key position has been filled.

If you are overqualified, the employer may be willing to upgrade the position or pay a higher salary if you sell yourself properly. You will have to convince the employer that he will be better off with a more experienced person like yourself. If possible, try to point out what he may save in time or in dollars by bringing in a more senior person.

Multiposition ads placed by large companies

Even if the positions advertised are for candidates with technical skills or expertise you don't have, chances are good the company may be hiring support staff as well. If you take the initiative and call the contact listed in the paper, your reward may be an interview for an unadvertised position for which there is little competition.

Positions with a relocating company

Only a certain percentage of employees are likely to be transferred to the new location, and once management is in place, new staff are likely to be hired even for positions not advertised. You can get a jump on other candidates by contacting personnel at the new branch or division. It's smart to research the products or services of the division or branch of the company that's being relocated so you will be better able to sell yourself to the hiring manager.

No matter what kind of help wanted ad you are responding to, it's smart to enclose a cover letter with your resume. Explain why you believe you are particularly qualified for the job, and state your strong interest in an interview. □

DROP IN FOR AN INTERVIEW?

Q: Is showing up at an office and asking for an interview on the spot a viable job search strategy?□

A: That approach works best if you're looking for an entry-level job or one in which there is high turnover (retail salesperson, fast-food worker, or cashier, to name a few). Of course, the manager who makes hiring decisions has to be in–something you may be able to determine with a phone call. You're also likely to fare better if you're the kind of person who makes a good first impression because you know how to dress, talk, and behave. An outgoing personality and a willingness to be able to handle people who may treat you rudely is also a plus in going with this approach.

Arriving unannounced on an employer's doorstep is generally not advisable if you are looking for a professional position in a traditional industry where appointments are expected. The exception: sales positions which require making cold calls on clients. If you have charm and the gift of gab, you may be able to talk yourself into an interview–and a job.□

GUIDELINES FOR PASSING OUT BUSINESS CARDS

Handing out your business card at social functions is fine if you do it with finesse. Here's how: After you have a conversation about your job search with someone who indicates they may be able to help you, it's smart to offer your card or ask for his or hers. You can also preface the gesture by saying, "Would you mind if I gave you my card? I sure would appreciate a call if you hear of anything."

But don't work a party the way you would a professional meeting or convention. It's obnoxious to turn every conversation around to your job search and evaluate the person you are talking to only in terms of their use as a potential contact. What's more, you may find yourself excluded from future social functions if word of your job mining spreads.□

SUMMERTIME JOB SEARCH STRATEGIES

While hiring generally slows down in summer, starting your job campaign while your competition is busy working on their golf game or tan can give you a big advantage. Here's why gearing your search up in summer makes sense and how to plan it:

● July is the beginning of many companies' new fiscal year, which often means new budgets, which may include money for hiring new employees.

● While there are fewer help wanted advertisements during the summer, employers are usually eager to fill positions that are announced. And because fewer people are looking, the competition is likely to be less intense. So spending your Sunday looking through the classifieds and writing cover letters to suit each situation can be time well invested.

● If you are putting off looking for a job because you do not want to give up your already scheduled annual summer vacation, keep in mind that you may be able to save it if you bring it up at the time you are offered a job.

● If you are a June graduate who has not yet found a job, take advantage of the more numerous temporary positions available as a way to get experience or your foot in the door of a company you'd like to work for permanently. Don't hesitate to recontact companies who haven't hired you about the possibility of filling in for vacationing employees. Or contact temporary agencies who specialize in placing people in the field you hope to go into.

● Develop a strategy. If you have not already figured out what kind of job you want to look for or who you'd like to work for, do that before you begin looking. Take advantage of the career information that can be found in most area library branches, including resume preparation books, books about specific careers, and directories of employers.

● Build your circle of contacts. You have to let people know that you are looking for a job if you hope to hear about openings through the grapevine. Summer activities—pool parties, barbecues, ball games, church outings, and club activities—are the perfect time to spread the word among friends and acquaintances you don't see on a regular basis.

● Plan on using some vacation time to job hunt. You'll raise fewer suspicions about your job hunt if you take off an occasional long weekend during the summer months. Mondays are preferable to Fridays because the employers you are calling are more likely to be in. If you are considering relocating, planning a vacation around scheduled interviews in that area is a smart idea.

● Be persistent with interview requests. Unless you are responding to a specific job opening, arranging interviews will probably require more follow-up than usual because of vacation or shortened work week schedules. A hiring decision may take

FINDING A JOB IN EUROPE

Finding a job in a specific European country is no easy feat. Unless you have dual citizenship, you must have a work permit, which the employer usually obtains for you. To get one, you have

to be better qualified than any other candidate in the European Economic Community, a group of countries where many well educated, highly qualified people live.

If you are a full-time graduate or undergraduate student, you can obtain a temporary work permit, which allow you to take local jobs for a period of up to six months in Britain, France, Germany and Ireland (and several countries on other continents). Contact the Council on International Educational Exchange, Attn: Work Abroad Programs, 205 East 42nd Street, New York, NY 10017-5706 (telephone: 212-661-1414). CIEE charges $160 for securing the permit.

If you're not a student, your best bet may be to write directly to companies located in the country you want to work in that are comparable to your current employer and/or likely to be in need of someone with your skills. The research librarian at your local library can help you locate the international directory of companies that best suits your needs. The library may also carry the International Employment Hotline, a private newsletter researched and written for job-seekers. If you want to subscribe, the cost is $39 a year; write to P.O. Box 3030, Oakton, Va 22124. The best opportunities abroad are in education, health care and other fields related to international development.□

FIVE INNOVATIVE STRATEGIES FOR FINDING "HIDDEN" JOB OPENINGS

In today's competitive job environment, it's easy to get discouraged because you may hear the "We're not hiring now" refrain more often than you do the top ten records on your favorite radio station. If you know how to look beyond the help wanted ads, however, you can increase your chances of getting interviews and a job that's right for you. Here are five innovative strategies that will help you uncover hidden job openings:

● Target growth industries. Cutbacks and layoffs often affect entire industries in a region or on a national scale, which is why it pays to think in terms of alternative types of employers. If you lost your job as a payroll clerk in the flagging construction or real estate industries, for example, it makes sense to look for work in a hot area such as health care.

The *Wall Street Journal* is full of trend stories that can help you learn which industries are expanding. Another source: the U.S. Department of Labor's magazine, *Occupational Outlook Quarterly*, which can be found in most libraries.

● Don't overlook small employers. Because they do not have the visibility that bigger, more established companies do, they are often overlooked by job hunters. How do you find out about them? Your local chamber of commerce can help provided you can tell them what industry or type of business you are most interested in working for.

● Anticipate openings by reading business stories. They contain numerous tip-offs about what the future holds for people in your industry and which employers are likely to be expanding their staff.

The advantage of knowing which parts of the economy are strong can help you identify employers you are more likely to get an interview with and also help you ask more intelligent questions when you are interviewing.

● Instead of applying to headquarters, try divisions instead. The fat staffs which were devoted to the administration of a company's business are getting leaner as top management has pared the ranks of middle management and given freer rein to those who manage their satellite operations. The message to job hunters: The pastures are greener for all types of jobs on the division level.

If you have come from a headquarters background, be sure to emphasize your flexibility and ability to do a number of tasks and point to examples of how you have been a problem solver—a highly prized quality with division employers who need "can do" types.

● Identify employers who sell their services to big companies. Small firms who do one type of work, whether it's data processing, human resources, or graphic design, are increasingly selling their cost-efficient services to companies who once did that type of work in house. If, for example, you used to plan your company's sales meetings, you should look for firms who specialize in doing just that.

For highly specialized functions such as meeting and convention planning, trade magazines such as *Successful Meetings* are packed with names of such firms. For more generalized functions such as accounting or tax preparation, you could check your local yellow pages.□

59
●

CONVENTION JOB-HUNTING PITFALLS

Conventions can be a great way to find out about positions that might be available with other companies. But it pays to be discreet because there's always a risk that you will be networking with people who are likely to be schmoozing with others from your company. Here's how:

● Be general rather than personal when talking to people you meet about the job situation at their companies. You are less likely to arouse suspicion if you mention what the hiring situation at your own company or department is like given the current state of business in your industry. The person or people you're talking to are likely to follow up with a comment about things in their companies.

● Avoid complaining or sounding down about your own job. That way, when you ask more specific questions, people won't automatically assume that you're job hunting. Finally, if you learn of an opportunity you might like to pursue and need to ask for specifics (the name of person to contact about it, for example), you risk less if you say something like, "That's sounds very interesting; I can't resist checking it out." Such a comment gives the impression that you're not around collecting leads from every Tom, Dick, and Harry.

● Realize that asking people you've just met or don't know well to keep your job-hunting efforts under their hat is like asking a stranger to watch your bag; there's no way of telling if they can be trusted.□

Q & A

HOW TO BEST USE A DIRECTORY OF EMPLOYERS?

Q: I have obtained a directory of people in a professional organization who often hire employees with my skills. I'm not sure if it's best to call them, introduce myself, and ask if they are in the market for someone to work on a full-time, part-time, or free-lance basis, or whether I should write a letter and send my resume. Any suggestions?

A: If the directory is not designed to be primarily for the use of its members (that is, it's available to people outside the organization), the most immediate way to make contact and get a response is to use the telephone. Most people are so busy that only the most conscientious take the time to answer a letter.

Before you make the call, practice what you plan to say. Ask for the person by name, explain where you got their name from, and briefly say what you do (public relations, customer service, or whatever) and ask if the person has a few minutes to talk about how you might be of assistance to the firm. You will probably be more successful if you get the person talking about problems or gaps they have in your area of expertise than if you start out by saying that you are job hunting.

A first question might be: "Is there anything you wish you could do more of or do better in the area of (graphic design, office management, or whatever)?" Listen carefully to what the person has to say, and ask for more details if the person comes across as talkative and friendly.

The more you learn about his or her problems, the better you can make your pitch about why you are someone worth hiring. If, for example, you find out that work is getting out late because no one knows how to set up a computer database, talk about your experience in doing that and suggest the person consider hiring you on a project basis. Be sure to follow up on any leads that seem promising with a letter, your resume, and eventually, another phone call.□

HOW TO GET THROUGH TO PEOPLE

Unreturned phone calls are the lament of every job hunter, but you should not feel put out when someone who doesn't know you isn't quick to get back to you. After all, you are the one who is asking the favor. You can, however, increase the chances of getting through if you do the following:

✔ Call before nine, after five, or during lunch time. You're more likely to reach your contact than his or her secretary, and you're less likely to find him tied up in a meeting or on another phone call.

✔ Get the person's direct number. If you first call the switchboard and then redial, you're less likely to be connected to a secretary's extension.

✔ Be authoritative. When someone answers the phone, say, "Mr. White, please," as if you're expecting that he's there rather than asking, "Is he in?" Another strategy is to announce your name, and say who suggested you call, which is especially effective if your contact and the person you're calling have a close relationship.

✔ Leave a message, but call back. Say who you are (and, if possible, who suggested you call) but also ask when it would be best to reach the person.□

HOW TO SHOP A JOB FAIR

Employers in some fields are discovering that too few job applicants are knocking at their doors, so many are trying to attract candidates at job fairs. These events, at which dozens of employers have booths, are often geared to recruiting people with skills in fields such as data processing, engineering, or nursing. But an increasing number are open to job hunters in a wide variety of fields, particularly those looking for entry-level jobs. Here's advice on how you can make the most of a job fair:

1. Get an advance list of the companies who are participants. They are sometimes listed in advertisements which appear prior to the job fair (check the Sunday help wanted section of your local newspaper). Or you can contact the organizer of the fair, which may be a company that specializes in holding them, or a college, consortium of colleges, or your local chamber of commerce.

There are two advantages of knowing who will be there: (1) You can make a point of getting to see your first-choice employers, and (2) you can do some preliminary research on companies that interest you so that you will come across as a stand out candidate when you meet their recruiters or managers. They will be impressed that you have done your homework and have made the effort to seek them out.

2. Bring up-to-date copies of your resume. At some job fairs, copying services are available at no charge, but it's smart to bring enough to hand out to all the participants. Another possibility at some job fairs is to pay a small fee (usually about $5) to have your resume put on a computer diskette that goes to all participating employers. One last option that's sometimes available to job hunters who cannot attend a job fair is to fax a copy of your resume for distribution to all employers or only ones that you specify.

3. Preshop job openings. At some job fairs, a survey of exhibitors and the positions they have available is listed at the entrance so that job hunters can make better use of their time. If that's not the case at the fair you are attending, it's best to tell a potential employer at the beginning of your conversation what you are looking for, or briefly describe your skills and ask whether the company has openings for someone like you . If you are willing to relocate, that's worth mentioning since an employer may not have the job you are looking for locally but may have a position in another location.

4. Act as if you are on a job interview. When you introduce yourself, speak clearly and confidently and extend your hand for a handshake (if it's wimpy and weak-wristed, practice with a family member until you develop one that's firm and friendly). You might start the conversation by saying where you currently work, what you are doing, what your skills are, and what you would like to be doing. Make your description brief and to-the-point. If you are looking for a specific position, say so, but be prepared to give a quick description of the job—job titles aren't usually good descriptors of the work involved, particularly in emerging industries and job areas. Then give the employer a chance to tell you whether his or her company might or might not be a good place for you to look for your next job.

5. Collect the cards of the employers you meet. While employers are likely to follow up with a phone call or letter if they are interested in you, it never hurts to let an employer know that you are interested. The letter can be short and to the point—you might reiterate your skills, provide another example of an accomplishment that's relevant to a job you would like to be considered for, or simply thank the employer for his or her time and ask that you be kept in mind.

6. Don't expect to get an on-the-spot job offer. While employers occasionally make spontaneous offers to people they don't want to get away, it's more likely that the human resources people who represent their companies will get back to you after they have had a chance to evaluate your resume. It's sometimes the case that line managers (the people for whom you will actually be working) attend job fairs and talk to prospective candidates, but even then, you will probably be asked in for further interviews before an offer is made.□

JOB HELP A RIP-OFF

Q: I have seen ads listed under "Professional Help" in the newspaper classified section. The firms want a $350 retainer and 3% of my annual salary if I obtain a job through them within sixty days. Are they legitimate?

A: Reputable placement services usually do not charge applicants; employers pay the fee if they hire a candidate introduced to them by the agency or service. If a placement service is geographically distant, that's cause for concern. Most employment agencies service employers and candidates in their area, unless they are national firms with offices in several cities.

It's not clear what you are getting for your $350; if it's a list of prospective employers, be wary; you can get the same information for free at a local library. One way to find out whether a company is reputable is to contact the Better Business Bureau in the county where the business is located. First, find out the company's address and phone number. The local BBB should be able to tell you whether they have received any complaints about that business. Another option is to ask for the name of satisfied customers you can speak with personally about their experiences with the placement service. If you don't get convincing feedback, don't waste your money.□

WORK AS AN INDEPENDENT CONTRACTOR?

Q: Is it a good idea to try to sell yourself to an employer by offering to work as an independent contractor?

A: Hiring a candidate as an independent contractor instead of a regular employee can be attractive to employers because they do not have to pay employee benefits to you or taxes, to government agencies. But the Internal Revenue Service maintains that you can only be classified as an independent contractor if: you have established your own business (and can show proof of this, such as a business license, business card or advertising, among other things); you have more than one client; you work out of your own office or pay rent to the employer whose premises you use; and you provide your own equipment and supplies. As an independent contractor, you are not entitled to collect unemployment or worker's compensation.

Employers who hire independent contractors and then treat them like employees are at risk because if, through an audit, the IRS claims their contractors are improperly classified, employers may be liable for legal fees, back taxes and penalties. You can be penalized by the IRS, too, unless you are fulfilling your tax obligations by filing your taxes (using a Schedule C) as a business owner.

If you have no real intention of setting yourself up in your own business, you would be better off registering with a temporary agency that places people with your skills if you want to try out an employer before you agree to come on board permanently.□

LEARN THE ART OF MAKING COLD CALLS

Making calls to prospective employers who don't know you is a skill that you can learn and improve if you follow these guidelines:

● Identify the best person to talk to. You're not going to get a receptive ear from most personnel staffers; it's far better to contact the person who manages the department you would like to work for.

● Write a script and rehearse it. It should be short and contain several elements: (1) An introduction (who you are and what you do)—for example, "My name is Linda Wells. I'm a paralegal with five years of experience in litigation." (2) An inquiry about the convenience of your timing—"Am I catching you at a good time?" (3) A brief statement about your accomplishments—"The research I have done has been used successfully by the partners I have worked for, in particular the XYZ case." (4) A request—"I've read that you are expanding your department and feel that my experience would help make the transition of adding new staff easier. Can we arrange a time to talk further?"

● Anticipate the objections of the employer and come up with counterproposals. For example, if the response is: "We're not interested in hiring anyone just now," you might ask if you can stop by to drop off your resume and introduce yourself.

● Put yourself in a sales representative's mindset. Be confident, not tentative. Be upbeat, not pessimistic. And don't take rejection to heart; you will hear "no's" much more frequently than a "yes," but if you make enough calls, you will get interviews.□

Q & A

OKAY TO NETWORK WITHIN COMPANY?

Q: My department was recently eliminated. At first, I was told that the company would try to find another position for me elsewhere in the company, but now the human resources people say there is no match. I've been tempted to call around to managers in other departments I've met and worked with. Would that be acceptable?

A: Absolutely—internal networking is a job hunting strategy that is one of the most direct ways to your next job. If your company's human resources staff is understaffed and overworked, as many are, it may not have turned over every stone. Besides, its staff members do not nearly have the level of motivation you do to locate new job openings.

If it's possible, try to stop by and personally visit with managers—a face-to-face meeting is always preferable to a phone call. Bring along an up-to-date resume *and* ideas about how your experience would be an asset to their department. Don't assume that people you've worked with know your strengths or background; they probably are only familiar with what you did on a particular project or in your capacity in the department that just disbanded.

Finally, don't forget to follow up phone calls or meetings. You may feel more awkward doing so once you are no longer on the premises. But these inside connections are valuable, and since you were a former employee, you already have the inside knowledge of how the company works—which can get you up to speed in a new job more quickly.□

HELPING AN EMPLOYMENT AGENCY HELP YOU

Working with an employment agency can be an important part of your job search strategy, particularly if you develop a good relationship with a counselor. The more you understand about how agencies work and the more information you are able to provide to a counselor, the more likely the two of you will be a successful duo. Here's what you can do:

1. Describe the kind of position you are looking for, and let the counselor know the level of responsibility and salary you would like. Then listen to what the counselor has to say about your marketability. Since counselors are in regular contact with employers, they are in a good position to assess whether what you are looking for is reasonable. Don't walk away if you don't like what you hear; instead, ask the counselor to explain his or her assessment and even to suggest ways you can improve your marketability. Consider the counselor's recommendations; after all, she can point out your weaknesses; employers usually won't.

2. Get back to the counselor about interviews you go on. Let him know how it went and whether you are enthusiastic about the company and the job. If the position was not right for you, tell the counselor why. The more information you can provide about the type of work environment, job responsibilities and people you work best with, the easier it will be for the counselor to send you on promising interviews. If the counselor continues to send you on inappropriate interviews, however, it may be time to switch counselors or agencies.

3. Don't waste people's time. If you are not serious about working for a particular employer, don't agree to a second or third interview. Doing so puts the counselor in an awkward position if you're offered the job and turn it down. And the counselor probably won't be willing to assist you further in your job search.

4. Keep the counselor informed about changes in your job status and requirements. Your counselor will appreciate knowing that you accepted a position elsewhere or decided to stay on in your current job—and be more enthusiastic about working with you in the future as a result of your consideration. It's smart to let the counselor know that you have modified your job requirements because it may open up possibilities he or she previously ruled out.

5. Pass along company literature. Once you are through looking over brochures or information that was given to you during an interview an agency sent you on, offer it to the counselor. She may like to add it to her files or read it over so that she can more knowledgeably speak about that particular client.

6. Offer to take on short-term assignments if the agency also places temporary employees. It's yet another way for an agency to get feedback about the kind of employee you are, which if it's positive, will cause counselors to be more invested in finding the right permanent job for you.

7. Don't forget to say "thank you." Regardless of whether a counselor is successful in introducing you to your next employer, it pays to make a call or drop a note to tell her you appreciate her efforts. Most job hunters don't bother to say thanks, which is why counselors remember the ones who do. And being remembered may be important in the future when the counselor comes across the next-step-up position that's perfect for you.□

PICKING THE RIGHT AGENCY

● Research which agencies are most likely to have jobs that match your experience and interests. Agencies generally specialize in one or more fields—engineering and computer science, for example, or clerical work. Advertisements that appear in the help wanted sections often mention the job or skill areas a particular agency handles. You can also check the yellow pages of a phone book for similar information. Then call the agency to confirm whether they have client companies in the industry you are looking in or work with job hunters with your background.

● Make sure the agency is reputable. Recommendations from friends or colleagues who have used it are valuable. You can also check to see whether it is listed in *The Membership Directory by Specialization of the National Association of Personnel Consultants*. The members listed subscribe to a code of ethics developed by the Association. The directory can be found in many universities and large libraries.

● Don't hesitate to ask questions about how the agency conducts business. Find out:
- how much training and experience the counselors at the agency have
- how they evaluate whether a job hunter and a client company might be right for each other
- what information they request from a client company about a job opening
- how many candidates they may send for interviews with a company

● Limit your agency selections. Rather than visiting a dozen agencies who specialize in your area, select a few. A counselor will be more likely to work hard for you if he or she knows that you are readily available for interviews and you have targeted that agency to help you find a job.

● Be wary of agencies that charge *you* a fee. Generally, employers pay the agency a fee when they hire someone the agency has sent.□

LEAVE A DETAILED VOICEMAIL MESSAGE

When you try to reach a contact by phone, you may well find yourself reaching the person's voicemail. That's why it's a good idea to rehearse what you want to say before you start dialing so you come across as self-confident. Here's what you should include in your message:

✔ Your name (spelling it is a good idea; even if you enunciate clearly, it's often hard for a person to "catch" what you said)

✔ Who suggested you call

✔ Why you are calling (remember: keep your request simple—"I hope you can give me advice about the best way to get an interview with your department manager.")

✔ Your phone number (repeat it, so the person gets it down right)

✔ Days and times when you are most reachable

✔ An acknowledgment that you value their time ("I know you're busy, but I'd really appreciate hearing back from you") and that you hope that you can someday return the favor☐

MOST JOB HUNTERS FLUNK THE "THANK-YOU" TEST

Ask anyone who has helped a job hunter out with a name, introduction, or advice if their help was acknowledged—the answer is usually "no." It's not only good manners but smart business to show your appreciation to contacts. Here's how:

1. Let them know that you'd be happy to return the favor. Even though contacts may be in a better position to help you now, you should tell them that, should the opportunity ever arise, you hope they will think to call you.

2. Thank each contact in writing. Sending off a short note within 24 hours of receiving help is a good practice; it shows you're on the ball.

3. Keep in touch with people you talk to. Since they've shared time and information with you, it's in your best interest to reciprocate by passing along news about what happened as a result of their suggestion or things you've learned that might be of interest to them. And, of course, be sure to inform all those who helped you when you land a new job.☐

HOW TO CONDUCT A JOB SEARCH LONG DISTANCE

ooking for a new job in an area of the country that better suits your lifestyle and pocketbook can be a good idea provided you follow these steps before you pull up stakes:

1. Give careful thought to your choice of a new geographic area. Any number of factors can influence where you think you want to live. It's smart to investigate whether your perceptions about these factors are well founded. A good place to start is *Places Rated Almanac* by Richard Boyer and David Savagean. The book ranks 277 metropolitan areas on factors including climate, housing, education, crime, prosperity, and transportation. Another useful book is *Finding Your Best Place to Live in America* by Dr. Thomas F. Bowman and others.

2. Get a handle on job prospects in your industry in the area you hope to move to. Start by asking questions of people in your field who live there—colleagues, friends, or clients. If you belong to a professional group, get the name of the person who heads up the chapter in the area you hope to relocate to.

You can also do some long-distance intelligence gathering by subscribing to an online service whose members often start professional special interest groups or forums. Some forums have job listings available for their members.

The Sunday editions of out-of-town newspapers (available in some libraries and newsstands) can further flesh out the employment picture.

3. Plan a trip to your new hometown and let employers and personnel agencies who specialize in placing people with your skills know when you will be in town. Once you have identified companies who hire people with your skills and background, send your resume and a cover letter that explains your interest in them and gives the dates when you will be visiting the area. (Note: You are likely to get a better reception from department managers than you are from human resources people.)

Say when you will follow up with a phone call—and do it. Your chances of getting in, even if no opening exists, are better simply because you are com-

ing in from out of town. (While you are there, check with real estate agents about the price of rentals or home purchases).

4. Be prepared to talk about why you are making a move. Many employers are wary of taking the risk of hiring a new employee who is relocating (the higher the salary level, the warier they are) because there is always the chance that you (or a family member) will not like the area as much as you thought you would. Because the cost of hiring and training a new employee is high, employers want to be reassured that will not be the case.

If you have past ties to the area (e.g., you attended college there) or have relatives living there, say so. Be prepared to discuss how quickly you can pull up stakes and make the move, too.

5. Allow more time than you otherwise would to find a job. Unless you have many potential job contacts in the new area, chances are your search will take longer because you are not as hooked into social and professional networks that produce job leads and information.

Decide, too, whether you want to cast a wider net and take a job that may not be as good as your last or current one. It may be a worthwhile tradeoff for getting established in a geographic area you want to be in.□

YOU CAN FIND A PART-TIME JOB

If you are among those job hunters for whom a part-time job would be ideal, take heart: An increasing number of employers are receptive to part-time arrangements because they realize that they need to accommodate the schedules of people who have skills that they need.

If you're already employed, the best place to start looking for part-time work is in your own "backyard." Even employers who have no policy on part-time work or who have never before tried it are more likely to be persuaded by someone whose work and reliability they know.

If that is not an option, keep the following things in mind in looking for part-time work:

1. The more in demand your skills and experience are, the better your chances of finding a part-time job. If you are a computer programmer, systems analyst, paralegal, nurse, or in any other high-demand specialty, you are in a good position to negotiate with employers.

2. Certain types of employers are more receptive to part-timers than others. The smaller the company, the more flexible management is likely to be about hiring a part-timer. Companies with nonunion work forces and those with progressive personnel policies are also more likely to be interested in hiring part-time employees. Hospitals, school systems, nonprofit organizations, and some state and local governments employ the largest permanent, part-time work forces.

3. Some fields and types of work lend themselves better to part-time work. Real estate, teaching, counseling, information science, research, writing, consulting, public relations, and health careers are among the areas where it's possible to function easily in a part-time capacity. Also, if the nature of your work is independent or project-oriented, you stand a better chance of making a part-time situation work for yourself and your employer. Jobs that require extensive client contact or managing staff make working part-time considerably more problematic.

4. Conduct your job search as if you were looking for a full-time job. You may rule out opportunities if you apply only for part-time positions or mention your time limitations in a cover letter. It's better to propose the possibility of reduced working hours during the interview, after you have had a chance to impress a potential employer.

5. Prepare a good case for how the arrangement would work. Take it upon yourself to come up with answers to the concerns your potential employer may have. In particular, talk about how the work will get done and scheduling problems solved. Talk about advantages for the employer and try to anticipate objections and provide evidence that these problems will probably not materialize.

6. Consider a job-sharing arrangement. If most of the positions you would want require a forty-hour-per-week effort or more, try to find someone with your skills, experience, and desire to work part-time and share the job. Then market yourselves to your current employer—or a new one—as a team.

7. Before you accept a part-time job, make sure you are not accepting a full-time job with part-time hours. Unless the responsibilities change, you are shortchanging yourself. Clarify fringe benefits. A fair deal is one which prorates benefits.□

SUCCESS STRATEGIES

PURSUE SECOND-HAND LEADS

If you know people who work for a company you'd like to work for, ask them about where the growth is in their company. Managers who head up growth areas sometimes don't even create job descriptions until they meet a person whose credentials and experience would help make their job easier or expedite growth even more.

When you don't know exactly what positions may be opening up, write a letter that stresses your top three strengths—your familiarity with a technical system, your sales track record or your ability to organize people. If your skills or experience are what's in demand, you may get a quick response. If you don't, follow up with a phone call to find out whether the information you received was accurate, or if you should redirect your resume.□

PLAY IT SAFE...OR PURSUE A DREAM JOB?

Q: I will soon be graduating from college and have participated in a few on-campus interviews with recruiters from companies outside the field I'd hoped to find a job in. I actually got a job offer from one. Since I have a lot of student loans to pay off, should I play it safe and accept it or try my luck at landing a job in the field I really want to be in?

A: You owe it to yourself to look for a job in your the field that most interests you because you will never know what could have been unless you try. Just because recruiters from your field are absent from your campus does not mean there are no jobs available. And you need not wait until you graduate to start your search. Use the resources of your career planning and placement office to identify potential employers. Ask for the names of alumni who are working in the field—they are worth contacting for information and guidance. You can start contacting employers now provided you have the time to follow up with phone calls and can schedule interviews.

Don't turn down the job offer you receive. Say that you aren't ready to make a decision yet, and ask whether you can respond to the offer after you graduate□.

CHAPTER 4

BEFORE THE INTERVIEW

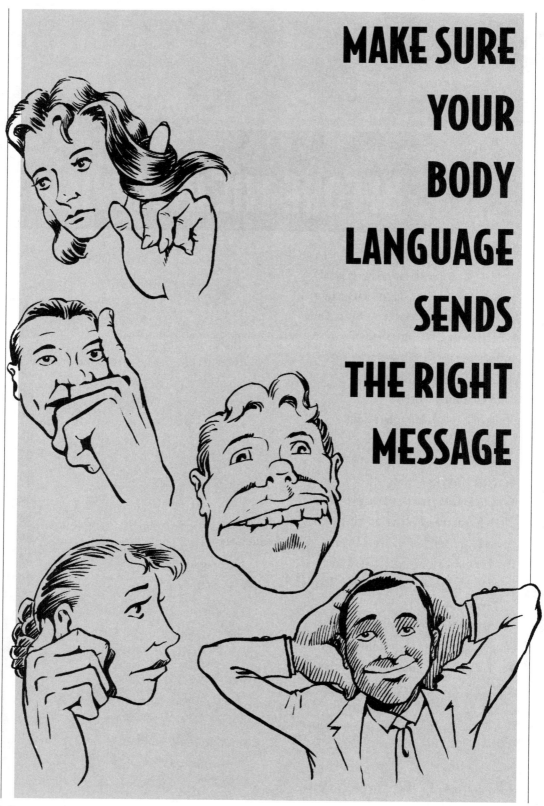

MAKE SURE YOUR BODY LANGUAGE SENDS THE RIGHT MESSAGE

No matter how composed you think you appear, it's a good idea to evaluate your interview body language and work at getting rid of or incorporating gestures and movements. Most people are nervous during an interview, and displaced energy needs to be controlled so that it does not detract from your presentation.

Before you can change anything, you need to become aware of what you are or aren't doing. A friend, relative, or colleague who is willing to be an honest critic can observe you as they ask you questions in a practice interview.

Another option is to videotape a practice interview. Since most people are more critical of themselves than are others, it's a good idea to have your "interviewer" rate your body language, too, and compare notes.

Here's what you should look for. Try to note (or have your interviewer note) when you are most likely to exhibit body movements you would like to change.

EYE MOVEMENTS

The big question is this: How often and for how long does your gaze meet the interviewer's? Good eye contact is critical to being viewed as a candidate who is self-confident and interested in the company and the job. Staring at the interviewer for too long a time or tracking his or her every movement can make the person feel uncomfortable.

What is desirable is making sure you are looking at the interviewer when he or she is asking you a question so it looks as if you are paying attention. When you are answering the question, try to maintain eye contact, too, although it's fine to momentarily shift your gaze elsewhere if you are pausing to look for the right word or gather your thoughts.

When the interviewer is speaking to you, maintain eye contact but break it by occasionally doing a slow blink and nodding or casting your eyes downward—doing so communicates you are thinking about something the interviewer has just said.

To be avoided: Rolling your eyes; squinting; rapid or too frequent blinking.

FACIAL MOVEMENTS

The best one, of course, is the smile. From the moment you shake hands (a firm, full grip is best) until you say good-bye, it's smart to do so often at appropriate moments. Smiling sends the message that you are relaxed and enjoying the conversation; it's also interpreted as a sign of self-confidence.

What moments are appropriate? Take cues from the interviewer. If he smiles, smile back. After he finishes describing the job (or at any other moment when a verbal response of interest or agreement is called for), try to smile when you say, "That sounds interesting," or "I see what you mean." Keep toothy smiles and ear-to-ear grins to a minimum.

To be avoided: Twitching your nose or mouth; licking, chewing on, or pursing your lips.

HEAD MOVEMENT

With the exception of an occasional nod (to show that you are following the interviewer's train of thought), it's best to keep your head erect and turned in the direction of the interviewer.

To be avoided: Tilting or rotating your head; tucking your chin.

HAND AND FOOT MOVEMENTS

Generally, the less movement, the better. When listening, keep your hands still by folding them on your lap or steepling (hands open, fingertips touching, almost as in prayer). If you are accustomed to "speaking" with your hands, do so but refrain from keeping them in constant motion. An open-palmed gesture (single or double) is a good way to emphasize a point.

To be avoided: Pointing your finger at the interviewer; drumming your fingers; gripping the arms or seat of your chair; wringing or clenching your hands; cracking your knuckles; pulling at your chin, nose or hair; jingling keys

or pocket change; folding your hands behind your head.

POSTURE

An erect but relaxed position is your best bet, which you can usually achieve by sitting all the way back in a chair and leaning slightly forward (from the waist).

To be avoided: Slouching; slumping; hunching your shoulders.

PERFECTING YOUR BODY LANGUAGE

Once you identify body language you would like to eliminate, it will be easier to do so. If it's a nonverbal behavior that's part of your normal repertoire, ask family members and friends to mention it when they see you doing it so that you can stop.

The best way to get rid of distracting interview mannerisms is within the context of a practice interview. Ask your interviewer to stop the interview if he or she catches you; do the same if you catch yourself. The more opportunities you have to do a practice interview, the more likely you are to incorporate positive body language into the script.

If you have used the videotape technique, save your first tape as a point of reference. When you feel you have made progress, make another tape and compare it. You will probably be surprised at the improvement.□

STRESS BUSTER

DON'T LET A BAD RECOMMENDATION HAUNT YOU

Looking for a new job can be made even more difficult if you feel pressure to do so because of a difficult situation at work or the circumstances of your departure from your last job were not pleasant. If you are worried that a former boss may hurt your chances of getting a new job by giving you a less than glowing recommendation, you can do things to protect yourself before your boss gets a call from a prospective employer. Here are some options:

● Ask for a letter of recommendation. Even if you left in a huff or on less than friendly terms, it does not hurt to ask, although an apology may be in order if your behavior was less than gracious. If your boss agrees to give one to you, chances are she will not later say something negative because she's already committed herself to positive comments on paper.

● If your boss refuses to give you a letter of recommendation, it's in your best interest not to list him as a reference. Instead, ask two people you worked with or for if they would be willing to act as references. If possible, line up at least one person who is at your boss's level or higher.

● Don't bring up the subject of a possible negative reference until it's necessary. Let a prospective employer get excited about you first. Remember, checking references is usually the last thing an employer does before extending a job offer, and sometimes it's even done after you are already on the job.

● Be frank about why you have not listed your immediate boss as a reference. If you didn't get along, it's best to couch a personality conflict in terms of a "difference in work style." You need not go into details; just offset the remark with two references from the same job who can speak well of you and your job performance.□

IT'S BETTER NOT TO USE A CHILDISH NICKNAME

Attention Bunny, Cookie, Muffy, Sonny, and anyone else whose childhood nickname still lingers:

If you want to project a serious, businesslike image, using your formal, given name is a good idea. Once you're hired, you can reassess the situation again. If it's a casual working environment and you are introduced to others who obviously use a nickname, you can always say, "Robert is my name, but most people call me Bo."□

GET A SNEAK PREVIEW OF A COMPANY'S DRESS CODE

Few companies have formal dress codes, but employees at every company do follow informal dress codes. If you want to be sure to fit the profile when you interview, pay a visit to the company lobby or premises at lunch time. You can discreetly check out what kinds of clothes are acceptable and define the company's image. If casual dress is sported by almost everyone you see, you may want to forego wearing a suit in favor of a more relaxed look. If all the men are in ties and coats and the women are in suits and dresses, however, you'll want to match that look on the interview. And keep this rule of thumb in mind: When in doubt, dress "up" a notch or two beyond what you might wear everyday on the job if you were hired.□

Q & A

BE PERSISTENT ABOUT GETTING AN INTERVIEW

Q: I recently responded to a help wanted ad by calling the employer. After I described my experience, which is limited, I was told I could not be considered because they were looking for someone with at least two years of experience. I would really like to work for this company and would like a chance to be interviewed in person. Should I call back and try to talk my way into an interview?

A: Definitely. There are two good reasons why it's worth your while.

1. The employer may change his mind about the number of years of experience he wants an applicant to have based on the response to his ad or the type of applicants he begins interviewing. He may discover that he's not offering enough money to attract candidates with experience, or the applicants who are responding have experience, but not exactly what he was hoping to find.

2. Calling back communicates an important message: You really want to work for this employer. But have your pitch prepared and rehearsed. You need to convince the employer that you are worth seeing in person because of the qualities other than experience that you can offer—that you're a quick study, highly reliable, very productive, and full of good ideas. You can probably increase your chances of being considered if you can get on the phone directly with the person making the hiring decision. Calling before nine or after five is the best way to catch the company president or department manager in.□

GET YOUR ZZZs THE NIGHT BEFORE THE INTERVIEW

Sleep, or a lack of it, can make a difference in how you well you do on an interview the next day. Here's how to insure a good night's rest:

● Do some kind of mild exercise after you have dinner—take a walk, ride a bike, or play in the yard with your children.

● Avoid drinking anything alcoholic; it can disrupt your sleep because you can awaken more easily during the night if you have been drinking.

● Do something relaxing before you go to bed: Listen to quiet music, read a book, or do breathing or imaging exercises to let go of the day's tensions and your apprehensions about tomorrow's interview.

● If you wake up and cannot go back to sleep because the interview is on your mind, get up and jot down your thoughts. What you write may be helpful the next day and, at the very least, getting your thoughts down on paper may make it easier to fall back asleep.□

SUCCESS STRATEGIES

HOW TO ACE INTERVIEW TESTS

Many employers feel that the only way they can tell for sure whether job candidates' credentials are what they claim they are is to test their skills, knowledge, and personal capabilities in an interview situation. You are most likely to be faced with a job test if you are applying for a position that requires using a particular skill, such as keyboarding, translating, or computer programming.

You can increase your chances of doing well if you take to heart the following guidelines:

1. Find out in advance whether a test will be given. If the prospective employer does not mention the possibility, ask. In addition to finding out what the test will cover, ask about the kind of equipment you will be working on and whether the test is timed.

2. Ask what a passing score is. It may be apparent in the job requirements, for example, a minimum typing speed of fifty words per minute. If not, find out. Most employers are quite willing to share that information because it saves them time to screen out candidates who do not have the minimum skill level. If what is expected is more than you know you are currently able to do, it's in your best interest to reschedule the interview to allow yourself time to improve.

3. Practice if the test involves a skill. Unless you have been regularly using the skill that will be tested, it's a good idea to brush up on it daily for at least a week or two before the interview. Try to simulate the test situation; practice on examples similar to what you would expect to be doing on the job. Timing yourself is critical if you will have to work under deadline in the test situation. Many business skills schools offer short, intensive skill refresher courses that may be worth investing in, if getting this particular job is important to you.

4. Rehearse "thinking on your feet." Some employers want to find out how resourceful, articulate, and knowledgeable you are during the interview. If, for example, you are a technician, you may be asked to describe how you would go about solving a theoretical problem situation. If you have reason to suspect that an interviewer may spring a "pop quiz," the only way to prepare is to come up with several different problems (they might be ones you have encountered in previous jobs or in schoolwork) for your interviewer to pose during a practice interview.

Ask a friend or colleague, preferably someone who knows something about the field, to play the role of interviewer. Your mission is to explain what you would do as clearly and succinctly as possible, while your interviewer should play devil's advocate.

5. Read up on the company and industry. The more familiar you are with recent developments in the company and field, and industry jargon, the more

easily you will be able to weave your knowledge into the informal testing that is part of every interview. Say, for example, you are applying for a paralegal position with a securities class-action law firm. If you are able to mention major decisions or ongoing cases, or, better yet, demonstrate an understanding of the issues involved, you will be several steps ahead of other applicants.

6. Follow directions carefully with a take-home assignment. If you are applying for a job that involves creative, analytic, writing, or research skills, you may be asked to respond to a set of problems or circumstances you might encounter on the job. Whether the interviewer gives the directions orally or in writing, be sure you understand exactly what he or she wants before you leave the interview.

Don't hesitate to ask questions about the factors that will be evaluated so that you can concentrate your efforts. If, for example, you are critiquing a presentation that was made to a client, find out whether an analysis of the budget is as important as an analysis of the ideas or the delivery system. Put effort into making your written report as clean and easy-to-read as possible; a sloppy presentation can cause you to lose points or even lose out altogether. Be sure, too, to find out when the employer expects to see your completed assignment.□

LONG COMMUTE A PROBLEM

Q: I am interviewing for jobs in a city that is a three-and-a-half-hour round-trip commute from my home. I don't have a problem with it, but several interviewers have questioned my willingness to travel so far. Is there anything I can do to make sure my commute doesn't interfere with my being offered a job?

A: Definitely. Prospective employers probably have several concerns beyond your willingness to put up with a long commute for months or even years—they may be fearful that you won't show up on time or at all if the weather is bad, or that you will be unable to stay beyond your normal quitting time when you're needed.

You cannot control the weather, of course, but you can say that you're willing to make up days or time that you miss when that happens. Or if it's possible, you might suggest that you are willing to work from home (and explain how you're set up to do so) if weather is likely to delay you for hours.

You should also stress your willingness to work late whenever it's necessary; if a friend or relative lives nearer work than you do, you can say that you have the option to stay overnight whenever it's necessary.□

TIPS ON FILLING OUT JOB APPLICATIONS

Filling out a job application is something most job hunters quickly tire of, but doing a careful job is important. Even small mistakes, such as misspellings and omissions, can ruin your chances of being considered for a job. Here's how to make sure yours is considered:

✔ Write legibly. If your handwriting is difficult to read, print. Use a pen with an even ink flow and a fine point (ask to borrow one, if necessary).

✔ Spell every word correctly. If you're not a great speller, take along a pocket dictionary you can refer to.

✔ Follow directions carefully. Pay particular attention to whether you're being asked to rank your preference of jobs or check off those you would be willing to accept.

✔ Proofread your completed application. In particular, look for misspellings or questions you may have overlooked.□

IS MAKEUP A MUST?

Q: I have never worn much makeup, nor do I care to. A friend of mine hinted that the reason I may not be having luck finding a job is that I don't have a "polished" look. I'm looking for a job that involves dealing with the public, but I feel my ability to communicate and put people at ease is more important than whether or not I choose to wear makeup. On the other hand, I really need a job. What is your advice?

A: You are right; your ability to do the job is more important than your appearance. On the other hand, the reality is that appearance does matter to employers. The question of what constitutes a "polished" look is highly subjective; one employer may feel that your lack of makeup is just fine, while another may not.

If the way you dress and wear your hair is appropriate for the industry and type of job for which you are applying, your preference of little makeup will probably not be an issue. If you are not sure whether your overall appearance is a help rather than a hindrance in your job search, ask friends whose professional image you respect for suggestions. The bottom line: You have to decide what if any changes are worth making.□

SUCCESS STRATEGIES

IDENTIFY JOBS WITH DIVERSE RESPONSIBILITIES

If you're a wiz at using a computer to accomplish administrative tasks, whether they involve word processing, database management, desktop publishing or money management, you may often get stuck with assignments that require that kind of expertise. If you'd prefer to spend more time in a new job performing a range of responsibilities, it's important to identify employers who are likely to give you more diverse job responsibilities.

One of the best ways to do more than what you're currently good at is to target small employers—those with 50 or fewer employees. Job descriptions are more general, and you will find that you can get involved with a number of different job functions AND learn the business. The more you know, the more promising your future job options.

Another strategy: Ask at the interview whether others in the department have software skills comparable to yours. A "yes" answer is an indication you won't be the only one expected to handle projects that require using those programs.□

PRACTICE MAKES FOR A PERFECT INTERVIEW

When the call or letter inviting you to come in for an interview arrives, you will be ecstatic. But that initial euphoria often gives way to preinterview anxiety. What if you are asked questions you do not anticipate? Or your nervousness causes you to talk too much? The best way to calm interview jitters is to do what actors and actresses do before they go on stage or in front of the camera: rehearse.

Conducting a practice interview is also valuable because it forces you to articulate answers, not just think about what you might say. By giving yourself a chance to edit and perfect your script, you will give yourself an edge over candidates whose "lines" are spontaneous. Here are some guidelines to help you make the most of a practice interview.

1. Ask a family member, friend, or colleague to play the role of interviewer while you play yourself. The more the person knows about the kind of work you do, the better. It's also helpful to choose a person who has been through the interview process—the more recently, the better.

2. Prepare a set of questions for the interviewer to ask. Many books about job-hunting and interviewing contain lists of the most commonly asked questions. You might want to add ones that you anticipate being asked in view of your job level or history, or your industry.

Be sure to include tough questions that get at the heart of why you are a good candidate for the job. If, for example, you are returning to work after having cared for your children at home for a number of years, a good question would be: "What makes you think you can handle the pressure that this position would often put you under?"

3. Think through what you are going to say in advance. You might even want to answer questions out loud to yourself to get the phrasing right. Try to come up with examples (when appropriate) to support what you say. If, for example, the question is: "What do you feel you bring to the job that other candidates may not?", you might respond by saying: "I can wear many hats, and I don't mind doing that. When I was a manager at X company, I often helped my staff collate and staple reports that had to get out by a certain time."

4. Act as if the practice interview is the real thing. Set up an environment that mirrors an interview environment—two chairs facing one another, or a chair facing a desk and chair. Go through all the formalities you would in a real interview, from the "hello" to the "good-bye" so that you practice all the important things—handshake, eye contact, body language, and conversation.

It's a good idea to dress in the clothes you plan to wear (particularly if you have never before worn them or rarely wear them) so that you can adjust anything that is uncomfortable or distracting to the interviewer.

5. Ask your interviewer to critique your performance. Tell him or her to note distracting verbal and nonverbal behavior, especially nervous habits—rubbing your hands together, saying "ah" or "um" too frequently, not looking at him or her when you speak. Encourage the interviewer to jot down notes about answers that could be clarified, expanded, or changed to help your presentation.

Instruct the interviewer to wait until the interview is finished to discuss his comments. Ask the interviewer to start the critique by telling you what you did well. Every job hunter needs the reassurance that he is doing something right.

6. Consider video taping your session. If you do not feel too intimidated by the presence of a camera and camera operator, put your camcorder to good use. The advantage is that rather than having the interviewer tell you what he or she thought, you can see for yourself how you come across. Most people tend to be too harsh on themselves, which is why it is important for the interviewer to balance your self-critique with his or her thoughts.

Have the camera operator keep the camera on you at all times. Closeups are good, but make sure the camera operator also gets your full-seated profile. You may want to have one practice interview before you try taping the interview so that you feel more confident.

Try not to focus on things that cannot easily be changed (the size of your nose or the pitch of your voice). But do look for body language problems you can correct (a swinging leg, twirling your hair). And be sure to listen carefully to the content of your answers and how well you expressed them. Both can be improved with practice.

7. Rehearse more than once. After your first runthrough, take time to decide what you are going to do differently, and work on your responses or behavior before trying again. Do as many practice interviews as necessary (with different interviewers if you'd like) to feel comfortable.□

TALK TO AN EMPLOYER BEFORE THE INTERVIEW?

Q: I was recently contacted by a company whose help wanted ad I had replied to. The secretary asked if I was available for an interview on a particular day. I thought it would be mutually beneficial to talk more about the job before I came in for an interview, and asked her to pass along my request to her boss. She seemed a bit put off, and I have not yet heard back from the employer. Was I wrong, and should I pursue it?

A: Smart employers do not want to waste their time talking to someone who is not truly interested. Unfortunately, the secretary who was scheduling appointments was too harried or not concerned enough to understand that.

If you are at all interested, by all means call back. Ask to speak to the person who is conducting the interviews. You may have to resort to calling before nine or after five to get that person on the line. Start the conversation by thanking the person for having selected you for an interview. Then say that because you realize he (or she) must be busy and do not want to unnecessarily take up his time, you would like to ask a few specific questions about the position. They should, of course, be knock-out questions, that is, questions that will easily help you determine whether the job is right for you.

If you see a problem, simply say what it is, for example: "It seems that the position will not involve supervisory responsibilities, which is something I am looking for." If, on the other hand, the employer's responses whet your appetite, state that you are very interested and why your experience is right for the job. Then schedule the interview.□

SUCCESS STRATEGIES

WELL-RESEARCHED IDEAS CAN HELP YOU IN JOB INTERVIEWS

The more you know about a company, the easier it will be to come up with suggestions on how it might improve its products, services, image or work processes. If you hope to work for the type of business that constantly needs a fresh supply of ideas, such as a magazine, advertising agency, or publishing firm, tailor your ideas to fit the audience or needs of the particular organization. If possible, try your ideas out on someone who is in a position to judge whether you are on the right track.□

HOW TO DETERMINE IF YOUR JOB SEARCH EXPENSES ARE TAX DEDUCTIBLE

CHECKLIST

You can deduct expenses related to a job search on your taxes if you have itemized deductions in excess of the standard deduction. Here's how to determine that:

1. Add up your medical and dental expenses, then subtract 7.5 percent of your adjusted gross income from them, which will give you your net medical expenses.

2. Add your state and local income taxes, and real estate and personal property taxes.

3. Add your interest deductions, which include deductible mortgage interest and points and investment interests.

4. Add up your gifts to charity, casualty losses, and moving expense deductions.

5. Add up job search expenses. They can include: typing, printing, preparation and mailing of a resume, career counseling, long-distance phone calls, and transportation and other travel expenses incurred on a trip whose primary purpose is to seek new employment.

Add up the totals from each step, then subtract 2 percent of your adjusted gross income. If that amount exceeds the standard deduction, you can claim your job search expenses.

There are exceptions to who may claim job search expenses. If you are a career changer, looking for a first job, or have been unemployed for some time, you cannot claim them. In one case, a schoolteacher who advertised for a job tried to claim that expense as a deduction on her taxes and was denied it because she had not been employed as a teacher during that year.

It's probably difficult to decide in advance if you will be able to claim your job search expenses for a particular year. That's why it makes sense to document them the way you would any business expense. Collect receipts and write down the purpose of the expenses on them. Expenses for which you do not have receipts should be logged into a diary.□

SUCCESS STRATEGIES

PAY FOR LUNCH IF YOU'RE ASKING FOR A FAVOR

If you have lunch with a contact who is sharing advice or information with you, the gracious thing to do is to pick up the tab. You should offer to do so regardless of who initiates the lunch since you are the person who stands to benefit the most from the meeting. Research the restaurants near the contact's office to find one that is quiet and moderately priced. Then call the person back, and say you would like it to be your treat and that you will be happy to make a reservation at a time that is convenient to him or her. If the contact insists on treating you (unbeknownst to you, he may feel he owes the person who suggested his name a favor), accept and let him choose the restaurant.☐

REVEAL YOUR SALARY REQUIREMENTS IN ADVANCE?

An employer calls in response to your resume and cover letter and says: "Before we talk about setting up an interview, I want to know what your salary requirements are so that we don't waste each other's time." What do you think is the most appropriate response?

A. I'd like to meet you and convince you that I'm the right person before we start talking money.

B. I'm hoping to get a salary between X and Y, but what's an even bigger consideration to me is the job itself.

C. I'm currently making X, and I wouldn't consider any position that didn't offer an X percent increase in pay over that.

D. Perhaps you could tell me what the salary range for the job is first.

The best answer is B. By naming a salary range, you leave room for negotiation and you communicate that you're interested in a good job match. Even if your range was higher than the employer's, he might have given you the benefit of the doubt and asked you in for an interview anyway.

Responding with A is likely to put off the employer; if there are other similarly qualified candidates who indicate that their salary requirements are in the right range, you may not get a call for an interview. A "C" response can come across as arrogant and inflexible, even if it is the truth. A "D" response may put off the employer because it puts him or her on the spot (even though it's an advantage for you, the job hunter, to know what salary range an employer has in mind).☐

TAP FORMER MENTOR FOR HELP?

Q: Several years ago, I worked for a company where I had a boss who I really considered a mentor. I am job hunting once again and would like to call and ask for his advice, but I'm embarrassed to do so because I never called to congratulate him about promotions I'd heard he'd gotten. Should I call anyway?

A: By all means—someone who has taken an earlier interest in you is one of the best contacts to tap when you are job hunting. Your former mentor will probably be happy to hear from you. You can start your conversation by congratulating him and telling him that you have continued to follow the progress of his career. Bring him up to date on what you are doing, and tell him that you are interested in his advice.

Let him take the lead from there; he may suggest having lunch or ask you to call back at a time when he's less busy. Be sure to thank him in advance of his help, and afterwards.□

HOW TO COME ACROSS AS A SERIOUS JOB HUNTER

DO'S & DON'TS

If you're not sure you want to leave your job but would like to see what else is out there, here's how to avoid giving the impression that you're "just looking."

DO give some serious thought about what you want to do before you start interviewing. Analyze what it is about your present situation that is making you unhappy—the lack of challenge, the hours, the pay, the commute, your relationship with your boss or coworkers.

DO rank your complaints on paper and write down how you would like each to change; you will have a better handle on how to proceed.

DON'T mention the fact that you're planning to look around to co-workers. Word may get back to your boss and jeopardize your current job situation.

DO pinpoint industries, companies, or jobs that would be an improvement over your current situation. Talk to people who work in those industries or jobs and do research in the business or careers section of your local library.

DO polish your interviewing skills. Have a friend or family member act as an interviewer and ask you questions including: "Why do you want to leave your current job (company, industry?)" and "Why do you want to work for a company (industry) like ours?" If you can give thoughtful answers to such questions, you will come across as a serious candidate.

DON'T be premature in your attempts to schedule interviews. Until you've done all of the above, you won't be ready to proceed.□

WHAT YOU SHOULD KNOW ABOUT HONESTY TESTS

More than 5,000 employers are using pen-and-pencil integrity or honesty tests to screen out applicants who are untrustworthy, according to a 1990 study done by the Congressional Office of Technology Assessment. Most private employers can no longer give polygraph (lie-detector) tests to screen job applicants—their use has been outlawed by Congress. The exceptions are federal, state, and local governments and private contractors involved in government intelligence or national security work.

You are most likely to be asked to take an honesty test if you are applying for a job with a bank or financial service business, a supermarket, hotel, fast-food restaurant, retail store, a manufacturer, or a hospital. At this time, you have little choice but to take the test if you want to be considered for the job, although psychologists, members of Congress, and civil libertarians are concerned with their potential for misuse. Here's what you should know about them:

TYPES OF QUESTIONS

Overt integrity tests pose straightforward questions such as: "If you saw another person stealing on the job, would you turn that person in to the boss?"; "Have you ever just thought about trying to steal something from any place?"; "Do you believe cheating people is worse than stealing money?"

Another type of test, sometimes referred to as a personality test, poses disguised-purpose questions such as "Do you make your bed in the morning?" or "How often are you embarrassed?" You may also be asked to answer "True" or "False" to questions such as "You love to take chances," or "You would never talk back to a boss or teacher." To detect inconsistencies in responses, tests often pose the same question in a slightly different way.

In addition to examining an applicant's propensity to steal an employer's money or property, some integrity tests are also used to forecast "counterproductivity," a term that is used to cover lateness, abuse of sick leave, absenteeism and even excessive personal use of the office telephone.

VALIDITY OF TEST SCORES

Test publishers and employers who are fans of honesty tests believe they provide reliable information about a person's predisposition to steal or engage in counterproductive behavior that costs the company money. Skeptics question whether honest people who fail the tests are unfairly knocked out of the running for a job. The OTA study, "The Use of Integrity Tests for Pre-employment Screening," reported that the existing research did not conclusively show that tests can reliably predict dishonest behavior in the workplace..□

HOW TEST SCORES ARE USED IN HIRING

Reputable test publishers urge client companies to use test results in conjunction with other screening strategies including the interview and reference checks. But the OTA study says that, "Whether these admonitions are followed in practice, however, is questionable...."

Unlike other types of personality tests that are given to job applicants, honesty tests are sometimes scored and interpreted by the employer rather than the test publisher, another factor that skeptics feel can be lead to misuse, particularly if test results are the dominant or sole criterion for selection.

WHAT YOU CAN DO

Before you take a test, you can ask the employer how test results are weighted. Any employer whose hiring decision rests on your passing it is probably not the kind of employer you want to work for. You can ask for the results to be shared with you; test publishers advise employers not to do so, but you will not know a company's policy unless you ask.

Finally, it's smart to provide any prospective employer with a reference sheet of former employers (complete with title and phone number) so that he or she can easily do a background check.□

HOW TO PREPARE FOR A ROUND OF INTERVIEWS

Interviewing by committee is common at many companies. Before you go through a round of interviews, be sure to:

✔ Find out exactly who you will be interviewing with—and how their positions are related to the one you're applying for. Ask how long each interview will last.

✔ Ask your main contact at the company what role each person has in the hiring process. Everyone may be expected to offer an opinion, but the decision may be up to one individual.

✔ Get information on each person you will be talking to. You may discover that you share the same alma mater or have something else in common. One way to get information is through a friend or ex-colleague who now works for the company. If that's not possible, ask your main contact if he or she can give you some background on each person.

✔ Whenever there are a few minutes in between interviews, excuse yourself to collect your thoughts or to freshen up.

✔ Prepare in advance a list of reasons why you are the best candidate for the job and a list of questions about the company or department.□

CHAPTER 5

THE INTERVIEW

HOW YOU SPEAK CAN AFFECT YOUR JOB CHANCES

Peter Jennings, Tom Brokaw, Connie Chung and other newscasters would not have their jobs if they did not speak with authority and conviction. Voice is not as critical a factor in many other types of jobs; still, you will be taken more seriously as a job candidate if you make an effort to get rid of speech patterns that convey a lack of confidence.

If your tone of voice sounds like you know what you are saying and you mean what you say, the person listening to you will find you more believable and impressive.

If you are not sure whether you are guilty of the following speech patterns, ask your spouse, a good friend, or a close relative to monitor your speech and alert you to violations. Once you realize what you are doing and when you do it, you can practice the solutions suggested after each problem pattern.

PROBLEM: Speech crutches. If pauses in your speaking are punctuated with "ah's," "um's," "you know's," or "like," you will not sound in control of your thoughts.

SOLUTION: When you are not sure what you are going to say next, say nothing. A silent pause is better than a speech crutch.

PROBLEM: Ending a statement on an "up" note. It makes you sound tentative and sends the message, "Is that what you wanted to hear?" A silent pause suggests more confidence than do speech mannerisms that paint a figurative picture of you shifting nervously from one foot to another.

SOLUTION: Practice ending any statement you make on a "down" note by dropping your voice as you say the last word or syllable of the sentence.

PROBLEM: Hesitation, especially starting statements or answers to interviewers' questions with "Well," "Hhmmm," or another speech crutch.

SOLUTION: If you need a moment to think, do it silently and begin your answer with a strong "I" plus an action verb, for example, "I graduated," "I completed," "I succeeded."

PROBLEM: Mumbling. If you do not clearly enunciate your words, you will be thought of as unsure of yourself.

SOLUTION: Try opening your mouth wider when you speak; it will help the words to come out more clearly. And

use your tongue, teeth and lips to help you articulate sounds. Imitating the diction of newscasters can help you improve.

PROBLEM: Speaking too softly. If an interviewer has to strain to hear you, chances are you will be written off as too timid. There is nothing wrong with a soft voice; it can be soothing and used effectively in many jobs. But do make sure you can be heard.

SOLUTION: Project your voice by speaking from your diaphragm, not your throat.

PROBLEM: The speedster's dilemma. Talking too fast is often a sign that you are nervous or trying to get the conversation over with as quickly as possible because you find it difficult or unpleasant.

SOLUTION: Practice speaking more slowly, articulating your words, and using silent pauses instead of speech crutches.

PROBLEM: The sing-song syndrome. If the rhythm of your voice makes your words sound more like a nursery rhyme than a statement, you will come across as childlike.

SOLUTION: Try to accent fewer words.

Finally, remember that no other candidate has your unique qualifications and experience. If you sound as though you value what you have done, the interviewer is likely to agree.□

HOW TO COME ACROSS WELL IN A PHONE INTERVIEW

Coming across well in a phone interview requires a different approach than that of an in-person interview. Here's how to handle such an interview:

☎ Ask if you can schedule the interview for a later time or date. Interviewers who call you at work understand that you may not be able to have a private conversation. Even if you get the call at home, it's to your advantage to put it off until you have had time to prepare.

☎ Make up a list of questions to ask the interviewer. If you ask intelligent questions that indicate your interest in the company, you will be more favorably regarded than a candidate who doesn't ask any.

☎ Write down your key credentials. In a prescreening interview, employers often focus on "knockout" questions, those that immediately disqualify you as a candidate if answered incorrectly. Such questions include, "Do you have a degree in X?" If you don't, but you cite experience that's equally valid, you can still fare quite well—something that's easier to do if you have already identified your strengths.

☎ Find out how long the interview will be. Before the interviewer starts asking questions, ask how much time he or she has so that you will not be caught short if you want to add information or ask questions.

☎ Avoid long-winded answers. Try to be specific, and make your examples to the point.

☎ Try to sound energetic and confident. Since the employer does not have any visual cues to go on, she will be trying to imagine the kind of person you are from your tone of voice.

☎ Rephrase the interviewer's question if you are not sure what he or she means. Inexperienced or incompetent interviewers do worse on the phone than in person, which is why you should not hesitate to clarify the question.

☎ Push for an in-person interview. If the job appeals to you, don't hesitate to say so, and ask if it's possible for the two of you to meet to discuss matters further. If the interviewer will not promise that, find out when you can expect to hear from him and be sure to thank him for having contacted you.

Finally, it's a smart idea to follow up with a note expressing your interest in the job and in an in-person interview.□

THE TOO-TALKATIVE INTERVIEWER

If you're unlucky enough to get an interviewer who won't let you get a word in edgewise, try these strategies:

1. Make a comment about your background or qualifications that feeds off a comment the interviewer has just made. If, for example, he says the position requires someone who is a stickler for details and who can work under pressure, jump into the conversation. You might say, "That sounds tailor-made for me." Then go on to give an example of why.

2. Interrupt with a question at an appropriate moment. It's particularly important to steer interviewers who get off on a tangent back on track with a question or comment about the job or the company.

3. Whether or not the interviewer asks, state several key points about your background or credentials that you want the interviewer to remember. You might say, "I'd like to briefly tell you why I think I would be a good candidate," even if you do not have a chance to do so until the end of the interview.□

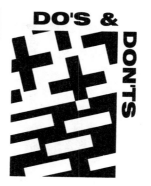

WHEN AN INTERVIEWER KEEPS YOU WAITING

It's not unusual to be kept waiting ten or fifteen minutes. But if an interviewer keeps you waiting longer without explanation, use the following guidelines:

DO ask how much longer it may be before the interview begins. If it's the case that you have another commitment or fear that the interview will be cut short because it's starting late, politely ask if you can reschedule the interview.

DON'T vent your frustration on the nearest employee—it's probably not the secretary's or receptionist's fault. Worse, she will probably report your remarks to the interviewer.

DON'T let your irritation affect how warmly you greet the interviewer even if he or she doesn't apologize for the delay. Put the waiting out of your mind and turn to what's really important—impressing the interviewer and finding out more about the job.□

RATE YOUR BOSS BEFORE YOU TAKE THE JOB

The position is what you have been looking for, the salary is a nice step up, and the company seems terrific. What sounds like the perfect job offer can be a booby trap, however, if you fail to evaluate your prospective boss.

You can learn a lot by asking questions during an interview and listening closely to answers. If possible, get additional input by talking to people who currently work for your prospective boss. Here are the factors you should consider in making an assessment of whether you and your potential boss are simpatico.

WORK STYLE — The more often you interact with your boss, the more important it is for your work styles to be compatible. It's particularly important to get a sense of how organized he is, the pace at which he works and how he delegates tasks, since all will influence how orderly or pressured your own work will be.

To get a sense of his work style, ask your potential boss to describe a recent project—how it came about, how the work was assigned, the kind of deadlines that were imposed, and how pleased he was with the results of the staff's efforts.

PERSONALITY — While it's not necessary for you and your boss's personalities to be similar, it is important to know whether you can get along. Most prospective bosses put on a good show during the interview, but you can get a sense of what a person's really like by noting several things.

First, does she laugh and smile easily? If she does, it's likely that she has a good sense of humor, one of the traits that is a cornerstone of a good boss/employee relationship.

Second, what is her style of questioning? The interviewer who fires one question after another without commenting on your answers is likely to be the kind of boss who issues orders the same way. It's up to you to decide if that's acceptable.

Third, does she seem happy with her job? If she lacks enthusiasm, chances are her dissatisfaction will affect you, too.

ACCESSIBILITY — Even if you are the kind of person who likes to work independently, it's important to know that your boss is there when you need him. Ask your prospective boss how he feels about staff coming to him with questions and problems.

How open he is to them is an indication of whether this is a person from whom you can learn or the kind of boss you hear from only when you have done something wrong.

EXPECTATIONS — You can get a handle on how demanding a person your potential boss is by finding out how she views the role of the person in the position you are interviewing for.

Ask how that person helps her do her own job better and how important that person's contributions are to the functioning of the department or business. By asking her to name the three things she most depends on that person to do, you will get a sense of her everyday expectations.

Notice, too, how interested your prospective boss is in you as a person as well as you as an employee. If she asks questions about your aspirations and seems genuinely interested in your answers, chances are she will be responsive to your needs.

JOB HISTORY — Most people like to talk about themselves and will be flattered that you are interested in finding out more about how they got to their current position. As your prospective boss answers questions about how he moved up you will get an insight into a number of things, including: his views on paying dues and promotions; whether he has a big-company or small-company mentality; how highly he values education or specific training; and whether he's conservative or innovative.

If, in the end, you sense that a good working relationship is not likely, it's smart to continue your job search.□

AVOID CHATTER; KEEP ANSWERS PITHY

Job hunters who don't know when to end a sentence can turn off prospective employers. Here's how to rein in your talkative tendency:

✔ Think through and rehearse answers to likely questions in advance. If you know what you want to say, there's less chance of rambling on than when you think on your feet.

✔ Keep your sentences short and to the point, that is, answer the question that was asked without giving too many examples or adding unnecessary detail.

✔ Prepare questions to ask the employer. If you catch yourself going on and on, you can gracefully exit from center stage if you have an appropriate question to ask

✔ Remind yourself to be a good listener. Don't forget to show you have heard and understood the interview by maintaining good eye contact, nodding, and repeating pieces of information.☐

BE HONEST ABOUT SALARY

Stating that your salary is higher than it really is can backfire: A prospective employer can usually verify it with your current or last employer or know from experience that it's inflated. Still, you are in a better negotiating position if don't name an exact dollar figure. It's acceptable to talk in terms of your total compensation package, which might include health or other insurance and stock options and other perks, as being in the low thirties, high twenties or mid-forties.☐

INTERVIEW QUESTION:

"WHAT KINDS OF PEOPLE DO YOU FIND IT DIFFICULT TO WORK WITH OR FOR?"

How to answer: Being totally up front about your personal likes and dislikes can work against you. Instead, say that you can get along with most people. Bring up an example of a difficult person you worked with, and talk about how you learned to deal with him or her. The important thing to stress, particularly in a preliminary interview, is that you are a good people person and have the skills and experience to work with a variety of personality types.☐

BEING A GOOD LISTENER CAN BOOST YOUR INTERVIEW PERFORMANCE

Many job hunters rehearse what they're going to say before going to an interview. But just as important is knowing how to listen to an interviewer's questions. You will be better equipped to respond effectively if you follow these steps:

1. Clear your mind. Forget about how bad traffic was and leave thoughts about your problems in the reception area. Turn your attention instead to what you hope to accomplish in the interview.

2. Anticipate the interviewer's question. People speak at 125 to 175 words a minute, but the mind can process information much more quickly. Rather than weighing how you are going to respond, wait to see if you've anticipated the question correctly.

3. Resist internal distractions. They're likely to sneak in if you allow your mind to wander even momentarily. It's common to worry about your appearance during the interview, for example. However, since you can't do anything about it, it's best to push the thought out of your mind.

4. Don't let "hot-button" words sidetrack you. When the interviewer mentions certain words, for example, "boss," "salary," or "reasons for quitting," chances are good you will have an emotional response. Try to keep your mind on track by focusing on what the interviewer wants to know.

5. Ask for clarification when necessary. Paraphrase the interviewer's question ("Do you mean...?") when you are unsure of what she is asking or you need a few moments to collect your thoughts.

6. Listen "between the lines." By studying the interviewer's body language and paying attention to her tone of voice, you can often get better clues about his or her reasons for asking a question.

7. Answer questions directly and vividly. Use the interviewer's words or phrases in your response and get to the point quickly. The more descriptive the words you use—numbers, names, concrete objects—the more easily your listener can grasp and remember what you say. □

CHECKLIST

WORK SURROUNDINGS

The offices that you are interviewed in may be much different from your actual work space, so ask to see where you would be working. Be sure to notice:

✔ The location, size, and feeling of the space you would be occupying

✔ Whether you are in a smoke-free area or where you would have to go if you wanted to smoke

✔ The level of noise and activity and whether it feels comfortable

✔ The equipment and furniture that would be exclusively yours and those items that you must share☐

INTERVIEW QUESTION:

"WHAT ARE YOUR WEAKNESSES? "

How to answer: One way to turn this loaded gun question to your advantage is to mention one or two work habits that will probably be viewed as positive by many employers, for example, the fact that you're a perfectionist or a workaholic. Another approach is to mention job skills or work habits that won't affect your being hired for this particular job. A third strategy is to talk about skills or habits you're in the process of improving (and the steps you're taking to achieve that improvement). No matter which answer you give, be sure to keep it short and sweet. And then switch the conversation to your strengths.☐

DON'T VOLUNTEER TOO MUCH INFORMATION

SMART IDEA

Don't assume that an interviewer is going to ask about or even wants to know all the details of why you left or want to leave your job. If an interviewer asks about your reasons for leaving or wanting to leave, keep your answer direct, but short, sweet, and positive. You might say, for example: "My job was eliminated along with a number of others in a cost-cutting move, but I'm looking forward to putting the skills and experience I developed there to work for a new company"

If you resent having lost your job, resist the temptation to lay blame on your boss or the company; no matter how you word it, such laments always come across as sour grapes. And even if an interviewer asks more questions about the circumstances of your dismissal, keep your tone of voice even and your answers neutral so that you don't sound defensive.☐

CHOOSE YOUR WORDS CAREFULLY OR YOU MAY TURN OFF AN INTERVIEWER

You may have all the right qualifications for the job, but you can easily be ruled out as a contender if you answer or ask questions in a trite, inappropriate, or off-putting way. Try to avoid committing the following verbal "sins."

1. "I'll try to do the job." If you are asked whether you can handle certain responsibilities or tasks, it's a mistake to sound wishy-washy. Employers want candidates who have the self-confidence to say, "I can do it," without hesitation.

2. "I like working with people." The big problem with this overused statement is that it does not tell an interviewer anything meaningful about you. Be more specific and say exactly what it is you like doing with people—for example, selling, managing, or collaborating.

3. "I'm flexible." When this response is given in answer to the question, "Would you be interested in a job in X department?" most interviewers frown. While it pays to be open to closely related jobs or departments, it's damaging to come across as someone who will take anything that comes along.

If you're interviewing with an employment agency, it's better to admit that you're not familiar with the area the interviewer mentions and ask for her advice on where she thinks you will fit in. But if you are interviewing with an employer, it's smart to be specific about which job or area interests you.

4. "I didn't like or get along with my coworkers." If you bring this up in answer to why you aren't happy in your current job, you may raise a red flag. An interviewer might wonder whether it's you who has a problem getting along with people. If possible, keep your remarks about your coworkers confined to what you may not have liked about their work habits or performance that might positively impress an employer. You might say, for example, that you had little patience for people who would not get their work done on time.

5. "I don't work well with (or for) women." Admitting your bias can deal your candidacy a death blow, whether you are male or female. With so many women in professional and managerial positions today, you are precluding yourself from many job opportunities if you make such a statement.

6. "In high school, I ...." When interviewers pose the question, "Tell me about yourself," it's deadly to reach back too far into your past. Unless you are a recent high school graduate, an interviewer is not likely to care how well you did on your SATs, whether you were a member of an award-win-

ning debate team, or the captain of the football team. Start at a relevant jumping off point, which could be what you're currently doing, why you're looking for a new job, or even what your first job was and how that relates to what you're now doing.

7. "I couldn't stand my last job." Bad-mouthing your current or former employer will not win you any points with an interviewer. Every job has its downside, but bringing it up in an interview makes an employer wonder whether you are a chronic complainer and likely to say negative things about your boss or the company if everything does not go your way. Instead of reciting what was wrong, talk instead about what you would like in a new job situation.

8. "Thanks for your time." While most interviewers do appreciate your thanking them, it's far better to be specific about how they have helped you. You might thank them for their career advice, information about the industry they have provided, or other people they may have suggested you contact in your job search.

9. "What's up?" When you call back to find out where things stand, you're likely to put off an interview by using this casual conversational phrase. Instead, say, "I was calling to check on how far along in the hiring process you are." □

RECONFIRM!

Always reconfirm the date and time of an interview the day before; misunderstandings do occur, or an employer may forget to notify you of a last minute change in schedule.□

HOW TO GAUGE BOSS "NICENESS"

If you want to work for a nice boss, be sure to:

✔ Pay attention to how he or she treats colleagues and staff when you are in for an interview.

✔ Ask if you can speak to the person leaving the job. If he seems happy to share information, ask if you can buy him lunch or call him at home to ask some additional questions. He will probably talk more candidly outside the office.

✔ During the interview, ask your prospective boss what she most appreciates in the people who work for her—her answer should tell you a lot about her as a person.□

Q & A

HOW FOCUSED SHOULD YOUR JOB GOAL BE?

Q: Am I limiting myself too much by telling employers that I want a certain type of job in my field?

A: If you are a recent graduate or have only a year or two of experience under your belt, it's to your advantage to let an employer know what kind of job you would prefer, but add that you are flexible. The reason? There is usually more than one path to getting where you want to go, so a diversion from your original plan or first job may be fine, provided it's in an industry you want to work in.

Experienced job hunters who pursue a narrowly defined job objective may find themselves unemployed longer than they want to be. You will not come across as unfocused if you broaden your job search plans and give serious consideration to jobs your skills will transfer to.□

107

TELL AN EMPLOYER YOU REALLY WANT THE JOB

Interviewers are not mind readers, and they are positively influenced by candidates who make a point of telling them that this is the job they have been waiting for. In fact, if an employer is trying to decide among several well-qualified candidates, the person who has communicated that he or she really wants the job is often the one who gets it.

The most appropriate time to tell an employer that you want the job is at the end of an interview. Don't be shy about it, even if it's not clear to you how serious a contender you are. You can simply say, perhaps as you shake hands, "I'm looking forward to hearing from you because this job seems perfect for me, and I feel I can contribute a lot to the company."

It doesn't hurt to express your interest again in writing. A thank-you note is always a good idea to send after an interview, and it allows you the opportunity to explain why you are enthusiastic about the job and the company. □

HIGH-RISK ACTIVITIES CAN HURT YOUR JOB CHANCES

Some employers (particularly those in innovative and new companies) are likely to think that physically dangerous hobbies such as mountain climbing and solo sailing indicate positive things about your character—that you enjoy a challenge and understand the importance of going through checklists to make sure you are prepared.

But more conservative employers (those working for banks, insurance companies, and hospitals to name a few) may simply not understand what's worthwhile or enjoyable about pitting yourself against Mother Nature. And they're likely to be even less impressed if your interest is in racing cars or bungee jumping.

You'll have to judge for yourself whether interviewers are likely to see positive parallels between your free-time interests and the kind of person they want to hire. When in doubt, play it safe and bring up a less risky pastime.□

HOW TO SELL YOURSELF IF YOU HAVE BEEN FIRED

Getting fired used to mean only one thing—poor job performance. Today, however, being let go often results from a company reorganization, downsizing, merger, or takeover. You can improve your chances of finding the right job and getting hired if you follow these steps:

1. Try to mend fractured relationships. If you reacted badly to news of your dismissal, it's in your best interest to apologize for angry words since a prospective employer may want to check with your previous employer. You might be pleasantly surprised by your boss's support now that the firing is behind both of you. If a phone call or visit cannot undo a relationship that took a long time to go sour, try to contact others in the organization who thought more of you and your work.

2. Bring up the subject before the interviewer does. Waiting for an interviewer to ask about why you left your last job is usually more difficult than broaching the subject yourself. The language you use to describe your reasons for leaving is important, too. You might say, for example, "I'm no longer working for XYZ Corporation—things were not working out from my perspective or from my boss's."

3. Don't lie. There's no point in covering up the fact that your employer told you good-bye, not vice versa, because the truth may catch up with you. It's far better to be honest, but not apologetic. Even if you were fired for poor job performance, you can couch the situation in positive terms. You might say, for example, that you took on more than you could handle, which was the reason that mistakes occurred.

4. Focus on the future. Talk about why you are right for this particular job or company based on what you have learned about yourself from your last job experience. Offer thoughtful answers about what you have already done—or plan to do—to correct your weaknesses. And be sure to communicate your commitment to doing what's necessary to be a top performer now.

5. Don't ever think of yourself as a failure. If you believe in yourself, you are halfway to finding a happier job situation.□

IF YOU PAID FOR COLLEGE, SAY SO

SMART IDEA

Employers are impressed with candidates who have helped pay for their college education. Why? Because it is evidence that you're a highly motivated person and have already begun to acquire good personal organizational skills. Figure out the percentage you earned, so that you can drop it into conversation at an appropriate moment. If you worked part-time, you may even want to add a brief explanation of how you managed to maintain your grade point average.□

CHECKLIST

WHAT TO TAKE TO AN INTERVIEW

✔ Several copies of your resume

✔ A pen and small pad (if you need to write down important information)

✔ Your calendar (in the event you need to schedule additional interviews)

✔ Samples of your work or a portfolio, especially if you're in a field where showing what you've done counts

✔ Copies of your reference sheet with the names and phone numbers of people whom the employer can contact about your past work performance

✔ A large envelope, slim briefcase, or portfolio cover to carry your papers in□

CONVERSATION TIPS FOR "QUIET TYPES"

Some employers like to hire people who have reserved personalities. Still, it's important to act as your own best advocate in an interview. Here's how to make a good impression.

1. Practice giving detail when answering questions. Interviewers can be turned off by candidates who give one- or two-word answers. Push yourself to give an informative answer by giving an example or providing details.

2. If you're a soft speaker, project your voice. Sit up straight in your chair, take a deep breath, and look directly at the interviewer when you're speaking.

3. Smile. It can make a big difference in whether you're perceived as a quiet, friendly person or a quiet, cold person.□

"WHAT DO YOU LIKE AND DISLIKE ABOUT YOUR CURRENT JOB?"

How to answer: Start with what you like about the job itself. Single out the responsibilities you most enjoy and have been successful at doing. If you have a good relationship with your boss, the management, or your colleagues, say so. Make it a point to say what you like about the company itself; its parent-friendly culture, its mom-and-pop-type friendliness, or the lack of red tape when decisions need to be made.

Even if your job perks were great, don't spend too much time talking about them; your prospective employer may not be able to offer ones that match.

In talking about your dislikes, try to pick out those things that might be seen positively. One might be that you no longer feel challenged by your work. Be prepared to explain what you have learned and accomplished and why you're ready for something new.

Avoid voicing dislikes that come across as bad-mouthing or blaming your current or previous employer. For example, don't get specific about job responsibilities that you loathed; it may the case that they are part of the new job description.□

SUCCESS STRATEGIES

CONVINCE AN EMPLOYER YOU CAN DO THE JOB

Convincing an employer to hire you if you have never done the exact tasks that the job requires can be tricky. Here's how to make a strong case for yourself:

● Investigate what the precise job tasks are by talking to people who work in a similar position or who know about that kind of job.

● Look for analogies between the new job tasks and ones you have successfully done in other jobs.

● During the interview, don't talk about what you do not know or have not done; instead, focus on the parallels and the fact that you are a quick study.

● Give examples of how you have been able to learn new skills and routines when you have stepped into unfamiliar "territory" in the past.

● Speak with confidence. If you sound like you believe in yourself, an employer is more likely to believe in you as well.□

HOW TO HANDLE A ROMEO OR JULIET INTERVIEWER

Few interview situations are more distressing than finding yourself face-to-face with a prospective employer who is more interested in romance than in business. As the job hunter, you are vulnerable because you risk losing out on a job if you offend the interviewer, or putting yourself in an uncomfortable job situation if you do not discourage his or her overtures.

Here are some of the ways to discourage advances and keep would-be Romeo and Juliets at arm's length:

● Dress like a professional. If you look like you are dressed for a party or social occasion, your appearance may invite inappropriate comments. It's important to make a visual statement that your purpose in being there is to talk business, not discuss the interviewer's—or your—social life.

● Be friendly, but not flirtatious. Smiling and being a good conversationalist are smart strategies in a job interview. But you will invite trouble if you talk to the interviewer the way you would to someone in a social situation.

● Ignore inappropriate compliments. It's one thing for an interviewer to make a kind remark about how well done your resume is; it's another to say that you are very attractive. A quick "thank you"—even ignoring the comment if you are uncomfortable—is the best way to handle an inappropriate compliment. Then bring the conversation back to something that is relevant to why you are applying for or are qualified for the job.

● Assess out-of-the-office interview suggestions carefully. If the interviewer is part of the personnel department, not the person you will be working for, lunch or drinks usually is not the place where subsequent interviewing takes place unless you are being interviewed for a high-level position.

On the other hand, it's not uncommon for prospective employers to ask candidates to lunch (and sometimes breakfast) to talk to them on an informal basis. If your interviewer suggests drinks, be wary.

If you suspect that the interviewer has intentions other than evaluating you for the job, you can: (1) ignore the suggestion (especially if it's mentioned in passing) or (2) ask if another meeting in the interviewer's office would be possible or (3) suggest having lunch rather than drinks.

● Respond candidly but politely to direct overtures. It does not happen often, but if a prospective employer asks you for date or suggests sexual favors, you have nothing to lose by being frank. Say that you are married, involved, or not interested. Don't be apologetic; after all, it's the interviewer whose behavior is inappropriate, not yours.

You may kill your chances of getting the job, but that's preferable in the long run to having to fend off the person's advances, which are only likely to become more brazen if you are hired. If you are eventually offered the job, you will have to evaluate whether the potential for future come-ons is worth this job opportunity.

A final caveat: If the attraction between you and an interviewer is mutual, and you feel that exploring the possibility of a romantic relationship is more important than the job, it's fine to convey your interest but smart to take yourself out of the running for the job.□

DO'S & DON'TS

MEAL INTERVIEWS

Few prospective interviews cause as much angst as being invited to join your potential boss, members of his or her staff, or business colleagues for a lunch interview. You have to contend with the pressure of being a decent conversationalist and someone with Emily Post table manners. Here's how to avoid interview indigestion and make a great impression:

DO keep the purpose of the meal interview in mind. Your potential employer's motive is to size you up in an outside-the-office setting and to get a better sense of what kind of person you are. So it's in your best interest to be more relaxed than you were during the formal interview and to let your personality—your sense of humor, your opinions, your personal interests—surface in conversation.

DON'T order food that can foil even the best efforts at control: lobster, dishes with tomato sauce, fish that's not filleted, a hamburger with "the works."

DO order something light or skip the appetizer if you are feeling nervous.

DON'T put your elbows on the table.

DO eat small, bit-size pieces and

DON'T talk with your mouth full.

DO bypass an alcoholic beverage. If everyone else orders one and you do not want to be the odd man or woman out, order one, but do not take more than a few sips: You cannot afford to be too relaxed.

DO be prepared to think on your feet. You may be asked how you would solve certain work-related problems. Rather than saying you have never had any experience dealing with such matters or that you do not know, give a thoughtful answer that demonstrates that you are at least aware of the steps you would take to get the information you need to solve a problem.

DON'T hesitate to ask questions about the job or company. Even if the conversation has revolved around nonwork topics, a lunch interview is a legitimate occasion at which to bring up questions that have occurred to you since your initial interview.

DO thank your prospective employer for inviting you out and, if you are convinced you would like to work for him or her, reiterate your interest in the company and the job.☐

SMART IDEA

PROPOSE A TRYOUT

If you really want a job and you know you're up against stiff competition, tell the interviewer you're willing to prove that you're the right person. Suggest that you spend several days (a week at most) learning the job tasks and showing that you can do them. Or propose that you do a critique of one of the company's products or services or take on a small, short-term assignment. You'll have to decide whether it makes more sense to offer to do it on a nonpaying basis or to be paid as an independent contractor.☐

Q & A

HOW TO EXPLAIN JOB MISMATCH

Q: I was let go after eight months on the job because things weren't working out— a mismatch, according to my employer. How should I explain this to a prospective employer?

A: Be honest, but couch your leaving in a positive way. To do that, you must first figure out what went wrong and why. The key thing is to communicate that you have learned something from the experience and that you're a better employee for it. Most importantly, avoid blaming the employer or allowing any bitterness or disappointment to show.☐

INTERVIEW QUESTION:

"WHY SHOULD I HIRE YOU?"

How to answer: Explain why you feel you are qualified for the job (talk about your experience, specific skills, or academic preparation). Say that you feel you will fit in well with the team or office and give one or two reasons why. Emphasize your interest in the company and the job, not just in terms of how each coincides with your career interest but in terms of the contributions you feel you can make.☐

INTERVIEW CONFESSIONS THAT CAN HARM YOU

No matter how friendly an interviewer is or how good a rapport you feel the two of you have developed, you can damage or kill your chances of getting the job if you reveal certain things about yourself or your past job experience.

While it's important to be honest, you need not volunteer information if you are not specifically asked. If you are, be sure to avoid making the following statements:

CONFESSION 1: I did not get along with my last boss. Since the employer probably does not know what kind of person or manager your boss was, he or she may wonder whether it is you who has a problem—whether it's accepting authority or dealing with a particular managerial style or type of boss (perhaps one who is of a different gender, race, age group, or background).

SOLUTION: Find something positive to say about your last boss even if it's

something as simple as, "He always met deadlines." If you cannot get around mentioning your discordant relationship, couch it as a business or work style difference rather than a personality problem.

CONFESSION 2: I had to leave my last job because of personal problems. If the problems involved your health, drug or alcohol abuse, or a marital or family situation, an employer will either write you off immediately (a likely consequence in the case of the first two problems mentioned) or wonder whether you will be able to cope with future off-the-job stresses without their interfering with your ability to perform your job.

SOLUTION: Be straightforward about any situation that was beyond your control—a serious illness or death in the family or an accident that prevented you from doing your job—and describe your efforts to balance the needs of that situation with those at work.

If you brought the situation on yourself or were seriously ill (through no fault of your own), try to avoid bringing the subject up at all—it's likely to work against you. If, however, you suspect the employer will learn of it through a background check, it's probably better to defuse the situation by mentioning it and stressing that things are better now.

CONFESSION 3: I thrive on constant challenge in my work. It sounds like a positive statement, but it can undermine your candidacy. Unless you are applying for a senior-level position or one that requires putting out a lot of fires, chances are good you will be expected to do plenty of routine tasks. Employers are reluctant to hire people who they suspect will become easily bored.

SOLUTION: Express your enthusiasm for taking on challenges, but in the same breath, talk about your willingness to handle the day-in and day-out responsibilities the job requires.

CONFESSION 4: My efforts were not appreciated or properly rewarded by my last employer. That may be the case, but mentioning it can make you come across as a prima donna. Furthermore, bringing up the topic of being under-paid or passed over for promotion will make you sound like a whiner.

SOLUTION: Talk about your accomplishments instead, and be sure to point out times when they were appreciated by your boss, management, or clients.□

STRESS BUSTER

CALM INTERVIEW JITTERS

1. Distract yourself from what is about to occur. Reading a newspaper or book is likely to take your mind off the impending interview. (Be sure to bring along a wet wipe for your hands if you opt for a newspaper.)

2. Engage the receptionist or secretary in conversation, provided he or she is receptive and not too busy. You may pick up valuable information about the company or the interviewer in the process.

3. Do simple meditation—close your eyes, sit erect, and breathe slowly and deeply. Imagine yourself in a carefree environment—the beach, a hammock under the stars, or on a sailboat.

4. Don't re-rehearse what you want to say during the interview; like studying for an exam, that's best done the night before.□

WHO TO "WATCH" IN A GROUP INTERVIEW

Watch the person who is speaking or asking a question—it shows that you are listening. But it's smart to occasionally turn your gaze to see how others are reacting; it will help you respond better to what's being said. When you are speaking, you should acknowledge everyone by shifting your gaze from person to person.□

EXPLAIN LONG SEARCH

Q: When interviewers ask me how long I have been looking for a job, I am afraid that if I am honest (it has been several months), they will think something might be wrong with me. How can I avoid giving that impression?

A: Don't sound apologetic or defensive. Mention any offers you have received, and say that you have not accepted them because you felt the fit was not right. Most interviewers are aware of how competitive it is to find jobs at your level or in your industry. What they are often interested in finding out is whether you are a go-getter and are as concerned about locating the right offer as they are identifying the best applicant.□

QUIZ

HOW WOULD YOU ANSWER THIS INTERVIEW QUESTION?

What do you expect to be doing in five years if you were hired?

A. Say you'd like to be in your boss's job

B. Say you're not sure

C. Say you'd like to be putting the skills you've learned on the job to their best possible use

D. Suggest that you only see this job as a stepping-stone

The correct answer is C. What the interviewer wants to know is whether you plan to make a serious commitment. Saying you're not sure won't help; saying you'd like his or her job can be threatening.□

"WHY DO YOU WANT THIS JOB?"

How to answer: It's important to be honest; most employers can see through candidates who try to fake their enthusiasm. But one of the following responses should work well for you—and make a good impression on the employer.

● Stress the satisfaction you get from doing this kind of work. If the job is something you enjoy doing, or think you would, say so. People who like what they do are likely to stay on the job longer and do their jobs better—big pluses for employers.

● Say that you want the chance to apply what you know and learn new skills. Emphasizing your ability to do the job is smart; saying that you hope to learn more shows you are a motivated individual.

● Emphasize the challenge of playing a role in making the organization function even better or improving the bottom line. Employers like to hear that you want a position so that you can do something for them.

● Be enthusiastic about the opportunity to work for this particular employer. If the job itself doesn't excite you, but you feel it's a way to get your foot in the door, talk about the positive things you have observed or heard employees say about working for the company.□

DO'S & DON'TS

HOW TO SELL YOURSELF WITHOUT BRAGGING

DON'T hesitate to talk about yourself and your accomplishments—you are your own best spokesperson.

DO talk in specifics rather than generalities. Instead of saying nice things about yourself (I'm smart, dependable, honest), talk about situations on past jobs or in school that demonstrate these qualities.

DO state the facts and use details. For example, you can say, "You can count on me to be here on time everyday. On my last job, I had the best attendance record in my work group."

DON'T spend too much time talking about yourself. Take cues from the interviewer. If he or she asks more questions, answer them. But if the interviewer does not seem too interested in hearing more, change course and ask a question about the job or company.□

INTERVIEW DRESSING

First impressions are based on appearance. So make sure yours sends the right message.

DO dress the part you hope to play: employee. Men usually can't go wrong with a suit and tie (unless the job always requires casual or outdoor clothing). A dress or suit is a woman's best bet. Making a fashion statement in a interview is fine if you plan to work in entertainment, fashion, advertising, or the arts.

DON'T wear a too-short skirt; it's distracting and unprofessional.

DO keep jewelry to a minimum. Simple earrings and necklace are fine; jangly bracelets can be distracting. Leave your nose rings and jewels at home.

DON'T sport a headset.

DO wear a watch.

DON'T bring excess baggage. Leave your coat, boots, umbrella, and briefcase in the reception area. Copies of your resume or other work-related material can be taken into the interview in a folder.

DON'T show up in athletic footwear.

DO choose a hairstyle that fits the image of the companies and industry you hope to find a job with. A trend-setting cut is fine as long as it will be seen as a plus by employers.

DON'T wear earrings if you're a guy, unless you know your employer would approve.☐

PACE THE INTERVIEW

When you are invited in for an interview, ask approximately how long it will last. It's advisable to verify the time before the interview starts—after you have exchanged introductions and pleasantries with the interviewer. A good way to put it is, "I realize you must have a very busy schedule. If you give me an idea of how much time we have for this interview, I'll keep that in mind as I answer your questions and ask my own." Then pace yourself so that you are sure to bring up what you want an interviewer to know about you in the allotted time. Your consideration will be greatly appreciated by the inter-

viewer because most candidates focus on their own needs, not the interviewer's. What's more, it shows that you're a professional.☐

WHAT TO FIND OUT IN AN INTERVIEW

✔ The job title
✔ The responsibilities
✔ Whom you will be reporting to
✔ Hours and days you are expected to work
✔ Your boss's work style (is he or she a look-over-the shoulder type or someone who expects you to solve problems on your own?)
✔ Whether overtime is required; if so, how often and the wages
✔ Whether travel is involved; if so, how often
✔ The salary or salary range
✔ Health benefits (deductibles, coverage, whether you are expected to contribute any portion of premiums)
✔ The career path or promotion possibilities
✔ Why the person who currently holds the position is leaving☐

HANDSHAKING

What's in a handshake? Plenty. Prospective employers form impressions about you as a candidate based on how at ease you are with this business greeting. Practice yours before an interview.

DO make sure your palms aren't sweaty. If necessary, keep a handkerchief in your pocket or purse and use it beforehand.

DON'T pull away too quickly (it will convey the impression that you're unsure of yourself).

DO grip the other person's hand. It doesn't have to be a knuckle breaker, but apply firm pressure (it's a sign of self-confidence).

DON'T pump. Shake up and down gently but firmly several times.

DO extend all four fingers into the palm of the other person and curl your thumb around the lower knuckle of the other person's thumb.

DON'T tone down your handshake when shaking hands with an interviewer of the opposite sex. Women don't like wimpy handshakes any more than men do.□

DID YOU KNOW...

WHAT TURNS OFF INTERVIEWERS

Job applicants who:
- Don't know when to stop talking
- Talk around questions instead of answering them
- Underestimate the interviewer's knowledge or experience
- Try to trip up the interviewer by asking technical or obscure questions
- Shamelessly name drop
- Question the interviewer's authority□

ILLEGAL INTERVIEW QUESTION:

"DO YOU HAVE CHILDREN OR DO YOU PLAN TO HAVE THEM?"

How to answer: Women are asked more frequently than men because they are still considered to be the primary caretakers. Employers are likely to ask because they are concerned that you may take time off if your child or caretaker is sick. If you feel that it's not the employer's business to know, you can say, "I have all my bases at home covered," or "My former employer can verify that I took no more than (or less than) the average days off." As far as plans to have children are concerned, you can reassure your employer by saying, "My career is what's most important to me now," or "If I do, I plan to return to work as soon as my maternity leave is over."□

WHEN AN INTERVIEWER SHORTCHANGES YOU

Here are four common worst-case interview scenarios and advice on what you can do:

THE DISTRACTED INTERVIEWER If the interviewer does not ask on-target follow-up questions or take notes, or allows frequent phone or staff interruptions, you might say, "I would be happy to come back if this isn't a good time." If your tone of voice is sympathetic, the interviewer may be relieved. At the very least, it's likely to bring her back to planet Earth and your conversation.

NOT ENOUGH TIME If the interview ends unexpectedly, say, "There is more I would like to tell you about my experience and qualifications," or "I have questions about the job that I was hoping you could answer." If the interviewer says, "We can do that the next time we see you," you will know that you are in the running. If his answer indicates there may not be another such opportunity, be on notice that your only choice may be to go directly to the person who will be making the final decision.

THE INEXPERIENCED INTERVIEWER If the interviewer doesn't have experience interviewing candidates or doesn't know enough about your area to ask the right questions, write a follow-up letter to the interviewer that explains why you are the right candidate. Say that you hope you will have an opportunity to meet the hiring manager.

THE SUBSTITUTE INTERVIEWER You do not find out until you have arrived that the person you were scheduled to meet with is unavailable because of sickness, an appointment foul-up, or an unexpected business development. Being seen by someone who is junior to your prospective boss is not only disappointing, it can hurt your chances of being hired. That's because chemistry and an interviewer's experience can play a major role in whether she is enthusiastic or blasé about you. Regardless of how well you think an interview went, it's smart to contact the person who will be making the final decision to request an interview with that person as well.□

SMILE, LAUGH, GET THE JOB

Mr Smiley? You're hired!

Not only can a good sense of humor help make looking for a job more a pleasure than a pain, it can also play a big role in how quickly you land the job you want. Ninety-eight percent of chief executive officers say they would hire a candidate with a good sense of humor over one who was straitlaced, according to a California State University survey.

You don't have to be a joke-teller or a stand-up comedian to have a good sense of humor. What counts is an easygoing attitude and the ability to see the lighter side of tough situations. Here are five suggestions on how humor can be used effectively in a job search.

1. Surround yourself with things that make you laugh. They could be cartoons about job hunting mistakes, resume bloopers, or insensitive interviewers. (One source is: *The Best Cartoons* from the *National Business Employment Weekly*, P.O. Box 300, Princeton, NJ 08543). Post them near your desk or telephone or on your bathroom mirror, or carry them in your wallet when you go on an interview. They can be great reminders that you shouldn't take any one phone call or person or interview too seriously.

2. Don't be afraid to "lighten up" in an interview situation. You will have to take your cues from the interviewer, but if she seems personable, make an attempt to get the interviewer to smile or laugh. Tell a brief story about something humorous that happened to you recently, but introduce the story at an appropriate moment.

One of the best ways to show that you have a sense of humor is to reveal something about your own foibles or faults. Employers often feel that people who are able to laugh at themselves make better team players or managers.

Save the jokes for friends; you risk putting off an interviewer whose sense of humor you're not familiar with.

3. Smile, chuckle, and laugh out loud. Responding to an interviewer's attempts to add a light touch or be funny can help cement the bond between you. If the interviewer is clearly trying to be lighthearted and make you feel at ease, feel free to join in the repartee by adding a comment of your own.

4. Mentally preview a comment or story before you speak. Spontaneous attempts at humor can work very well, but you should stop to think about whether they're appropriate in an interview situation. If you feel a glib remark fell flat, say so: "Looks like I bombed with that one." The interviewer will be less put off if you try to recover gracefully.

5. Look for a workplace that encourages humor. You can get a sense of how solemn or playful things are by employees' responses to being introduced to you. Visual cues, such as what's on department or employee bulletin boards, are also telling. According to business guru Tom Peters, "The number one premise of business is that it need not be boring or dull. If it's not fun, you're wasting your life." □

TALK ABOUT YOUR ACCOMPLISHMENTS

Whether or not an interviewer specifically asks about your past achievements, it's to your advantage to slip them into the conversation. The following items are evidence of a job well done.

Promotions, formal or informal. A change in job title or responsibility (whether or not it was accompanied by a raise) is a good indicator that you were well thought of by management.

Feedback from clients or customers. Letters or phone calls that complimented you on your helpfulness, effectiveness, or ability to get speedy results all speak well of you as a candidate.

Demand for your help. If you were more frequently consulted by colleagues or called upon by other departments than others at your level, you come across as someone who has a lot to offer.

Positive performance appraisals. Don't hesitate to cite specifics communicated to you in writing or conversation. Just preface your comment with, "My supervisor told me ...," □

WHEN AN INTERVIEW TAKES PLACE OUT OF THE OFFICE

DO be yourself. That's a tall order when you know your personality, behavior, and appearance are being evaluated by others. But trying to conform to an image you feel fits the job or to a group mentality you are not comfortable with will make you come across as a phony.

DON'T provide details about your personal life that may cast a negative light on your candidacy. It's natural for people to inquire about your family life and how you spend your free time. But it may not be in your interest to reveal that you are a single parent, care for an elderly parent, or are active in an organization that requires a lot of your free time—at least not before you are hired.

DO take conversational cues from others. If sports is the topic of the day, talk about your favorite teams or preferred activities. Don't be afraid to ask questions on the subject of your would-be colleagues; it shows you have an interest in their lives and opinions.

DON'T be too quick to down an alcoholic beverage. If everyone else is drinking and you do not want to be the odd man or woman out, order one, but nurse one drink slowly: Loose lips and behavior are likely to hurt your chances.□

IT'S RISKY TO CALL AN INTERVIEWER BY A FIRST NAME

Even if an interviewer calls you by your first name, it's best to continue using Mr., Mrs., or Ms., particularly if you are not sure which a female interviewer prefers. Your inclination may be to respond with informality especially if the interviewer is younger than you. But until the interviewer says, "Just call me Jack or Sue," it's better to be conservative than presumptive.□

SCRIBBLERS, TAKE NOTE!

Putting pen to paper during an interview is generally not a good idea; you risk putting off the interviewer because writing as you listen demands a shift in your attention. You will probably be able to remember most of the important things an interviewer tells you about the job if you jot them down shortly afterward. The exception to the rule about keeping your pen in your pocket: If the interviewer mentions the names and titles of key people or other critical information. □

"DO YOU HAVE ANY HEALTH LIMITATIONS?"

How to answer: If your health is excellent, you have nothing to lose by saying so. But if you have a health problem or handicap, you need not reveal it unless it would prevent you from doing a competent job. One way to deflect the question is to say you would be willing to take a health examination; a positive response is not likely to create suspicion. If you are subsequently denied employment for health reasons unrelated to your ability to do the job, you would have grounds to challenge the employer.□

SMART IDEA

KEEP MOONLIGHTING QUIET

If you advertise the fact that you spend your evenings at another job (even if it's an occasional avocation such as playing in a band), an employer who is considering you for a full-time day job may worry that you will be too tired to perform at peak level at your regular job. He or she may also worry that late hours may keep you from being punctual or prevent you from putting in necessary overtime.

So before you reveal the existence of your second job or your avocation, get the job, get to know your boss and the culture of the company, and prove yourself to be a conscientious and productive employee.□

Q & A

HAVE YOU MISSED OUT ON A JOB IF YOU MISTAKENLY MISS THE INTERVIEW?

Q: I missed an interview because I put it down on the wrong day in my calendar. Should I call and explain my mistake or have I blown my chances?

A: Call—you never know how an employer will react. He or she may be disappointed that you did not show because you were the most promising candidate on paper or the only one (it happens). It's best to say you made a mistake when you wrote it down. Apologize for any inconvenience you may have caused, reiterate your interest in the job and the company, and ask if it can be rescheduled□

REDUCE CHANCES OF UPSET STOMACH

It's normal to experience some kind of reaction to an anxiety-producing situation like an interview. For many, it manifests itself in an upset stomach, which can affect how well you come across in an interview. Eating light and easily digestible foods the night before the interview and for breakfast (or lunch) can help. Carry an over-the-counter antacid with you to an interview is a good idea too.

Finally, work at relaxing. A touch of nervousness can help you perform better, but too much can detract from how you come across. You can reduce stress by listening to your favorite music, reading a book you know you can get lost in, or doing progressive relaxation (closing your eyes, breathing slowly and deeply, and imagining a calm scene) just before you go in for the interview.□

CHAPTER 6

AFTER THE INTERVIEW

HOW TO KEEP YOUR SPIRITS UP WHEN YOU HAVE BEEN JOB HUNTING WITHOUT SUCCESS

The worst part about looking for a new job is that rejection is built into the process, no matter what your job level or experience. Even if you tell yourself that the employer who did not hire you is the one who is losing out, it's hard to keep your ego intact when all you are hearing is "Sorry, but we have hired someone else."

It's in your best interest to keep your disappointment from affecting your outlook; employers are quick to recognize people who are down on themselves (or the world) and are not likely to hire you. Here are antidotes to the job blues:

1. Keep your expectations in line. Most interviews do not result in an offer. Even if you are called back for a second or third interview and they go well, you cannot count on getting hired. If you do not make the final cut, take satisfaction in having made it as far as you did.

2. Don't take rejection too personally. Many times job applicants are rejected for reasons beyond their control—someone else had been hired unofficially, but the interviewer had to see candidates to satisfy company or government policies. Or budget cuts came into play and the position was taken off the market, after you already had an interview. Even if you suspect that you were not hired because the employer did not like something about you, don't worry about it: You are better off working for someone who likes you just the way you are.

3. Reward yourself. Looking for a job is often more difficult than performing in a job. The best way to keep your enthusiasm and energy level high is to treat yourself whenever you have completed a difficult task or day or get a rejection. It does not need to be something exotic or expensive, just something that gives you pleasure—renting a video, spending time with friends, or playing a round of golf. Getting your mind off your job hunt can help you face the next group of calls, letters, or interviews with a more positive mindset.

4. Connect with people who can empathize and offer constructive suggestions. Your family and friends can play this role for a time, but you will put less of a burden on them if you can find additional sources of support. Low-or no-cost job clubs, which often meet in churches, libraries, community organizations, or the offices of outplacement specialists and career counselors, are a good bet. If you cannot find one in your area, consider starting your own support group by posting a notice in a professional publication, a church or community bulletin, or even on a computer bulletin board.

5. Participate in activities at which you can excel or win recognition. Your self-image may be tied primarily to what you do for a living, but when you are not working, it's important to develop alternative means of establishing self-esteem. If you are a sometimes athlete, put yourself into a training routine. Volunteer to work on a committee, in a community or school organization, if possible one that requires you to use skills you have developed through your work. Another option: Enroll in a certificate or degree program. Classroom success can be a big ego-booster and provide important job contacts or expand your job skills.□

DOES LACK OF PERSONAL QUESTIONS SIGNAL AN IMPERSONAL WORK ENVIRONMENT?

Q: I have gone to six interviews with five different people at a company I thought I'd really like to work for. What bothers me is that not once did anyone ask anything about me as a person—my interests outside work, my family life, or where I live. Am I'm being overly sensitive in my view that this would be a cold place to work?

A: Your vibes about the company culture may be on target. However, it could also be a case of conservative interviewers trying to avoid asking illegal non-job-related personal questions. Most employers like to know more about job candidates than what they bring to the job. If that's your only concern about working for this company, try to get the names of employees who work for the company from family, friends, or business contacts. Ask them how they like working there; if others feel that the atmosphere is impersonal, you're likely to hear about it directly or by listening between the lines.

Another option is to ask to visit the department where you would be working, a request that's appropriate to make if you're offered the job. By observing how friendly and interested in you your prospective co-workers are, you can make a first-hand determination of whether the impressions you got through interviews are valid.□

SUCCESS STRATEGIES

HOW TO OVERCOME OBJECTIONS

When several people are involved in interviewing and hiring a candidate, you may get feedback from an "ally" about potential hurdles to your getting hired.

It's in your best interest to get as much information as you can about people's doubts. Say that you would like an opportunity to counter their objections and ask your ally for strategy advice. Find out if a phone call, a letter, or even another interview would be most appropriate. Then come up with good reasons or evidence about why these concerns should not stand in the way of your being hired. One common concern is whether you're serious about staying more than a year or two. It never hurts to explain why you're prepared to make a long-term commitment. How effective you are in convincing them that you can do the job can be a deciding factor in your getting unanimous approval.□

THE OFF-PUTTING INTERVIEWER

Q: At a recent interview, I was surprised and distressed to find that the interviewer was unfriendly and almost hostile. She made no effort to put me at ease and asked questions whose purpose seemed more to put me on the defensive than to find out information. I really wanted to work for this company, but now I'm unsure how to respond if I do get a call back for further interviews. What's your advice?

A: Interviewers who don't know the basics about conducting good interviews or whose interview behavior isn't professional do their company a disservice. It may have been the case that your interviewer was inexperienced or having a bad day herself. Or she may have wanted to see how you would respond under stressful circumstances, an interview strategy used to test those who are applying for jobs that require being able to handle such pressure effectively.

The bottom line: Be open to further interviews. If you discover that the attitude of the first interviewer is typical of future interviewers, including your prospective boss, you may want to reconsider whether the company culture is a good fit for you. If the interviewer is not the hiring manager, you might want to contact that person and ask for an interview. Mention that the first interview was not as productive as you would have liked, and briefly explain why you are a good candidate for the job.□

SUCCESS STRATEGIES

SET THE RECORD STRAIGHT

After you've had a chance to replay an interview in your head, you may decide that an answer you gave to an interviewer's question may have created a misimpression that could hurt your chances of getting the job. What can you do about it?

First, share the highlights of the interview with family members, friends, or colleagues whose opinion you trust. They may tell you that your concern is misplaced or on target. If it's the latter, it's wise to clear up the matter immediately. Write a short note to the interviewer and set the record straight. Apologize for any confusion your answer may have caused. And reiterate your enthusiasm for the job.□

WHAT TO ASK BEFORE YOU AGREE TO A TRIAL ASSIGNMENT

Marianne, a magazine editor with eight years' experience, provided three months' worth of ideas for future issues for a prospective employer. She did not get the job, and was upset when the person who did called her to ask if she wanted to write one of the stories she had suggested on a free-lance basis.

Joan, an account executive with twenty years' experience, was told that she had to prepare a marketing plan to be considered for a job. She did not get the job and was angry that her written work was not returned to her.

When the supply of job hunters exceeds demand for them, employers often ask for and get free help or expertise from candidates. Many such requests are legitimate; that is, employers feel they can make smarter hiring decisions if they have a chance to see how a person thinks or performs on the job. But you should carefully evaluate what you are being asked to do and why before you agree. Here's how.

1. Ask the employer what he or she hopes to learn about you as a candidate through the assignment or tryout. A thoughtful, sensible answer is an indica- tion that the employer is on the up-and-up. If the employer avoids responding directly to your question or cannot artic- ulate what role the assignment or tryout will play in the hiring process, beware.

2. Find out from the employer if others who are up for the job are being asked to do the same. The most favorable sce- nario is if the assignment or tryout is being requested only of the top candi- dates; then you know that the employer has screened candidates through tradi- tional interviewing techniques and ref- erence checking. If the assignment or tryout is being requested of all appli- cants, think further about whether it's worthwhile for you to go ahead.

3. Do a quick analysis of how much time or effort the assignment will require. If a day or weekend's time or more is necessary to do a good job, real- ize that you may be at a disadvantage if you're already working full-time. What's more, if that kind of effort is required, think about how you will feel if you make the effort and don't get the job.

If an assignment is going to take more than five hours, it's appropriate to bring up the question of payment. You might want to ask the same question if you are being asked to perform work for which you need no training. But realize that if other job hunters are willing to do so without compensation, you may put yourself out of the running by asking.

4. Determine whether the assignment is an exercise or consulting advice. Be wary of giving advice or providing ideas for what appear to be actual company problems. Exercises that show your thought processes or reveal your problem-solving abilities are, on the other hand, appropriate.

If you are someone with considerable experience or expertise in an area and are being asked for ideas that an employer could actually use, say: "I've made a nice career doing that exact thing for the companies I've work for. Are you willing to reimburse me for sharing that expertise with you?" If the response is "No," walk away without regrets; it's probably not a company where you would be happy working.

Should you provide a company with free ideas or advice, ask in advance who will see them, whether they will be photocopied, and whether the work will be returned to you.

If you have positive feelings about the company after one or more interviews, have a good feeling about the person who is making the request, and really want the job, trust your instincts. Impressing an employer with what you can do can be a deciding factor in your getting the job.□

GET PAID FOR A TRYOUT?

Employers sometimes propose that you work for several days or even a week so that both parties can judge whether the match is right. There are no hard and fast rules about pay. But be sure to ask whether you will be paid—and how much—at the time the tryout is mentioned or on the day you report in for work. Employers who do not plan on compensating people for tryouts often feel that it's a training session, which costs them or their employees time (to teach and evaluate you). And depending on the nature of the job, you may not actually do what could be called productive work.

The bottom line is this: If you want to be considered for the job and an unpaid tryout is a prerequisite, you have no choice but to agree. If, however, the tryout extends beyond a day's time (and presumably you would learn simple tasks that the employer would be paying someone to do), you should not hesitate to bring up being paid for future hours. If you're a quick study and are doing productive work, the employer should be willing to compensate you or make an offer. If he's unwilling to do either, look for a job elsewhere.□

DO'S & DON'TS

ACE FOLLOW-UP INTERVIEWS

Just because your first interview with an employer went well doesn't guarantee that you've got the job. Whether an interview is the second or the tenth one with a company, treat each as if it's the most important interview in the hiring process. Before you go into follow-up interviews:

DO ask who you will be talking to. Get their names and job titles and ask about their role in the hiring process.

DO find out from your first interviewer what other interviewers' preferences are in job candidates, so that you can be prepared to talk about what's most important to each.

DON'T play one interviewer against another. Even if interviewers' views of what your role would be differ, keep your thoughts and questions to yourself. Save them for the interviewer with whom you have the best rapport, and voice them at a time when a job offer is imminent.

DO follow up with each interview. Try to bring up something that particular interviewer considered important and that you feel you can address if you're chosen for the job.

SUCCESS STRATEGIES

MAKE A PUSH TO BE THE TOP JOB CONTENDER

After an interview with an employer you decide you want to work for, it's to your advantage to call the employer and let him know you are very interested in the job. Interviewers cannot always judge how interested you are in the position during the interview. And they are more likely to choose a candidate who really wants it. Because decisions often take weeks, it's also a good idea to stay in touch with the employer. You can make a pest of yourself with too many phone calls, but you can maintain your visibility by:

1. Sending articles you've clipped that discuss business issues of interest to your employer or that lend support to things that you may have talked about in the interview;

2. Passing along written comments from others about your past job performance—they may be letters from clients or job evaluations from your boss;

3. Developing a list of ideas or putting

together a business plan or strategy that you would like to implement if you were hired.

Making an effort to demonstrate that you're the best candidate can go a long way toward the employer making his or her decision in your favor.□

PUT JOB SEARCH ON HOLD WHILE AWAITING IMMINENT OFFER?

Q: After a series of interviews with an employer I would very much like to work for, I was verbally told a job offer was imminent. Two weeks later, I was told that it would probably be a matter of several more weeks before it was clear whether there would be money in the budget to hire me. Another four weeks have gone by. My would-be boss continues to say that he wants to hire me, but the funds have not yet been released and he cannot say when that will happen. I have put my job search on hold, thinking this job would materialize. Am I being foolish to do so?

A: Because money is tight and organizations are behaving more cautiously these days, hiring scenarios like the one you have described are becoming more common. But no matter how much you want a job or how confident you are about it being offered to you, it's short-sighted to reel in your lines before you have your prize catch in the bucket. And that is never the case until you have received a formal job offer, preferably one in writing.

So before any more time goes by, get back on the phone with employers you have contacted but not yet heard back from. Continue networking and developing new leads. If the job offer you are hoping for comes through, you have lost nothing. In the meantime, you may turn up another offer. With that in hand, you can go back to your first-choice employer. If that employer wants you badly enough, it may be just the right catalyst for that evasive job offer to materialize.□

WHAT "WE'LL GET BACK TO YOU" REALLY MEANS?

On one level, the phrase functions as a way to close an interview and as a social nicety. Unfortunately, the unspoken clause that follows those words is "if we are interested." While the words imply that the employer will make the next move, you should not be deterred from doing two things: (1) asking if the employer has a timetable for interviewing candidates and making a decision, and (2) checking back in to see where things stand if you do not hear back within a week or two. Be politely persistent, and at the very least, you won't be left "hanging."□

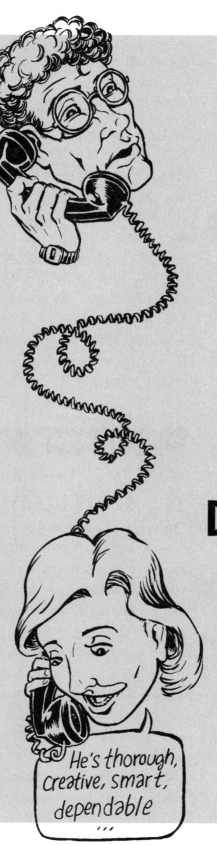

REFERENCES: DO EMPLOYERS REALLY CHECK WITH THEM?

iring decisions are based on candidates' qualifications, how well they come across in an interview, and what others, particularly former employers, colleagues, and even clients, say about them. Getting verification about your work habits and work style from people with first-hand knowledge is important to employers, particularly if you are applying for a position of trust.

What kinds of questions is a prospective employer likely to ask your references? Beyond the facts—how long you were employed and what your title was—employers may ask questions about your reliability, your integrity, and your productivity. Some employers, particularly those who work for large organizations, are very careful about giving out anything beyond factual information because employees have successfully sued former employers for passing along negative information about them. Still, that does not stop employers from making inquiries and getting the information they are after.

Some employers ask the references you have provided for the names of other people who may be able to comment on your performance, including clients or colleagues. It's during these conversations that discrepancies are likely to surface because these people have not been selected by the candidate. Even if this happens, the employer is not likely to base a hiring decision on what one person says, particularly if you have not been given an opportunity to respond.

Because you never know whether or how extensively a prospective employer will check references, it's important to be honest. Fudging on factual information, particularly academic credentials and honors, dates of employment, and responsibilities, is likely to get you into trouble because it is so easily verified.

If you feel something in your job history will work against you, you have to weigh whether to bring it up in as positive a way as you can, or let it go and hope it will not surface during a reference check.

Finally, it's a good idea to call your references after each job interview. Here's why:

● You can alert them about getting a call from a prospective employer. A reference who is expecting to hear from a prospective employer is bound to come across as more knowledgeable and supportive than is the reference who is caught off guard.

● You can clue the reference in on which parts of your experience are worth emphasizing. If, for example, your ability to take initiative is important to the hiring employer, ask your reference to make it a point to talk about occasions on which you did so.

● It gives you an opportunity to touch base and say "thank you" in advance. That's particularly important if you have not spoken to the reference in a while. You can also bring him or her up to date on what you have been doing, which can help the reference sound more authoritative in talking about you.□

WHAT TO DO WHEN A PROMISED CALLBACK DOESN'T COME

Q: An interviewer recently told me that she would get back to me by a certain date, but I've heard nothing. This isn't the first time this has happened. Why don't employers follow through on their promises? And should I take the initiative and call back myself?

A: There are a variety of reasons why you might not hear from an employer by a specified date: The person may have forgotten what she told you, the search time may have been extended, people who are part of the hiring decision may not have made up their minds or may have been diverted by more pressing business needs—the list can go on and on.

Sometimes employers promise to get back to you and fail to make the call because they are uncomfortable delivering the bad news that you will not be hired. It's not fair, and it happens more frequently than it should.

It never hurts to pick up the phone and call to check the status of a job search. Remind the person that she told you that she would get back to you (in a nice, not a confrontational way) and ask if the decision has been made. If it has not been, ask if you are still in the running and when a decision is likely. Finally, politely inquire whether the employer minds your calling back to check in at the time a decision is expected.□

SMART IDEA

FOLLOW UP WITH A NOTE

One of the simplest and easiest ways to boost your chances of getting a callback interview or a job offer is to let an interviewer know that you want the job—in writing. Your letter can be short and to-the-point; all you need to do is:

1. Thank the person for giving you the opportunity to meet with him or her.

2. Mention the particular skills, experience or personal qualities that will enable you to do the job well.

3. Say that you hope that you can meet the hiring manager (or whomever) or that you will have the chance to prove that you're the right person for the job.□

GET THE INSIDE STORY ON WHAT A JOB REALLY INVOLVES

One of the biggest mistakes job hunters make is accepting a job that they have not fully investigated. The result? Frustration and unhappiness may set in soon after you start working when you realize that the interviewer glossed over certain details and that you failed to ask enough questions. You can avoid the problem, however, if you make an effort to find out what a job really involves before you decide if it's right for you. You will probably have the opportunity to take these steps in a follow-up interview.

1. The best way to find out what a job is really like is to talk to the person who currently holds the job. Most prospective employers will not mind your doing so if you are a serious contender for the position, and you say that you want to make sure it's the right choice for both of you. If the employee has already left the company, talking to co-workers with whom she regularly dealt is another possibility. Try to find out:

● What's involved in the job tasks that have been described to you

● Whether there are additional hidden responsibilities

● How frequently specific job tasks must be done

● What the most time-consuming responsibilities are

● What the most pleasant and unpleasant aspects of the job are

2. Talk to future co-workers. How much you identify and get along with co-workers is likely to be a major factor in your overall satisfaction. So it's smart to ask your prospective employer to introduce you to the key people you will be interacting with. You can get a sense of how friendly they are and what their backgrounds are by asking questions including:

● How long have you been with the company?

● What are your responsibilities and how do they relate to the ones I might be assuming?

● What do you like most and least about working here?

3. Get a sense of the organization. You can find out a lot about its personality and philosophy by observing and talking to those who work there. How people dress and speak is one indication of whether it's a formal or informal workplace—information that's often unclear in a job interview.

You can find out what the pace of work activity is and whether employees enjoy what they are doing by noticing how relaxed or pressured they are in conversation or as they go about their work. The locations of people's offices provides some information about job status. Finally, you can reconfirm your impressions of what kind of person your prospective boss is by watching how people respond to her.

If you are troubled by something you have heard or observed, bring the matter up with the employer after you have been offered the job. She may be able to allay your fears or offer a concession that may change your mind.□

CHAPTER 7

THE OFFER

IS A NEW JOB WORTH MOVING FOR?

An employer has extended you a tempting job offer, but it involves moving. The issue of whether a relocation makes sense depends on a number of factors, each of which should be carefully considered.

This quiz can help you determine if the advantages of such a change outweigh the negatives. If you're single, answer the questions in Part One. If you're married or have a serious romantic involvement, have your partner answer the questions in Part Two. If you have children, take into account the factors described at the end of the quiz.

Rate each factor on a scale of 1 to 5.

5 = Definitely; **4** = Somewhat; **3** = No effect; **2** = Possibly; **1** = No

PART ONE

Before you start, read over the list of 20 questions and circle the five factors that matter most to you.

_____ 1. Will your salary be significantly higher?

_____ 2. Would your new job responsibilities be more interesting?

_____ 3. Do you expect to have a good working relationship with the person to whom you'll be reporting?

_____ 4. Will it provide opportunity to add significantly to your skills or expertise?

_____ 5. Does it offer good possibilities for advancement?

_____ 6. Will it involve better working conditions?

_____ 7. Does it represent a boost in job status or prestige?

_____ 8. Will you have better fringe benefits?

_____ 9. Will it provide better working hours?

_____ 10. Will you have more control over how you spend your time on the job?

_____ 11. Are you excited about the prospect of meeting new people and making new friends?

_____ 12. Will you be able to get comparable or better housing at an affordable price in your new location?

_____ 13. Will your new transportation costs be lower?

_____ 14. Will your state and local income taxes be lower?

_____ 15. Does the new location have cultural or recreational opportunities that are important to your lifestyle?

_____ 16. Will there be opportunities to socialize with people who interest you?

_____ **Total points**

Score A (remember to double the points for questions you have circled)

Are you reluctant to:

_____ 17. Move away from relatives?

_____ 18. Move away from friends?

_____ 19. Give up your involvement in church, civic, or community activities?

_____ 20. Give up your present housing situation?

_____ **Total points**

Score B (remember to double the points for questions you have circled)

_____ Subtract Score B from Score A and put the total here.

If you're single, skip the next section and go to the "Results" section. If you're married or have a serious romantic involvement, have your partner answer questions 21 through 30 in Part Two.

PART TWO

Before you start, read over the list of questions 21 through 30 and circle the two factors that matter most to you.

Are you reluctant to:

_____ 21. Move away from relatives?

_____ 22. Move away from friends?

_____ 23. Give up your involvement in church, civic, or community activities?

_____ 24. Give up your present housing situation?

_____ 25. Take on more household management responsibilities?

_____ 26. Are you fearful that you'll be the one who experiences a greater sense of loneliness and isolation in your new community?

_____ 27. Do you feel resentful about being asked to make the move?

_____ **Total points**

Score C (remember to double the points for questions you have circled)

_____ 28. Are your chances of finding a comparable or better job in the new location good?

_____ 29. Do you look forward to the prospect of living in a new place?

_____ 30. Are you excited about the prospect of meeting new people and making new friends?

_____ **Total points**

> **Score D** (remember to double the points for questions you have circled)

_____ Subtract Score D from Score C and put the total here
(note: your score may be a negative number)

RESULTS/PART ONE

If your total score was 81 or higher, you're a good candidate for relocation. Even though you may be worried about some aspects of a move, chances are good that the advantages will outweigh the negatives.

If your total score was between 61 and 80, you clearly have some reservations about changing your situation. If you've given a negative rating to any of your five most important considerations, it's a good indication that you may have problems with those aspects of your job or life if you make the move. That doesn't mean you shouldn't go ahead, but you should be aware of and prepare for those potential troublespots.

If your total score was 60 points or less, you'll be doing yourself a favor to pass this job offer by. Even if it's an improvement over your current job situation, you'll be better off looking for an equally promising situation closer to your own backyard.

RESULTS/PART TWO

If your partner's score was 5 or less, it's a good indication that he or she is as good a candidate for relocation as you are.

If your partner's score was between 6 and 15, you should talk over his or her concerns (the circled questions in particular). Unless your partner is positive-minded and feels capable of resolving them over time (with your help), you may want to think twice about relocating because his or her happiness is at stake.

If your partner's score was 16 or more, you can count on some major relationship strains if you make the move without addressing his or her concerns. Keep in mind, too, that it may not be within your power to compensate for the negatives your partner foresees.

ABOUT CHILDREN

While you and your spouse should make the final decision about whether relocating makes sense for the family, talking to school-age children about their feelings is a good idea. Changing schools, leaving friends or relatives, or giving up their participation in clubs or on sports teams can have a traumatic effect. If you talk about their feelings before you make your decision, however, you may be able to allay their fears and raise their excitement rather than their anxiety level.□

WHAT TO DO IF YOU LOSE OUT ON A JOB

The bad news that you were not the Chosen One is never easy to hear. It's in your best interests, however, to take the news gracefully and act on it. Send a short, carefully composed letter to everyone at the company with whom you interviewed and thank them for their efforts in supporting you. Wish them success with the candidate they have chosen. Then say that should things not work out the way they had hoped or if they decide to add a similar type of position, you would very much like to be considered again. Knowing that you're a good sport and that you remain interested in the company and the job can make a difference in whether you are recontacted in the future.□

HOW TO EVALUATE A JOB OFFER

CHECKLIST

In the excitement of getting a job offer, it's easy to lose sight of an important factor: Is it the right one for you? It's best not to rush back with an answer; most employers prefer deliberation to hastiness because they don't want to invest training time and money in you, only to have you change your mind. Here's what to consider before you give an answer:

✔ **The job itself.** If you're unsure of what the day-to-day work will be like, talk to the person who is currently doing the job you would be taking over. Your future boss may be able to tell you what needs to be done, but he or she may not know how it should get done. Those with whom you'll be interacting can also be a good source of information.

✔ **Opportunity for advancement.** Is this position going to prepare you to move into more desirable positions in the future? Finding out what employees who held the job before you have gone on to is the best indication of what your prospective career path is.

✔ **Stability of the company.** Even if it has been in business for a long time or has a good reputation, it's smart to find out whether its finances are in good shape and whether any imminent changes are likely. The business pages of the newspaper are one source of information; talking to people familiar with the company is another.

✔ **Who you work for and with.** It's important to like and feel you can function comfortably with your prospective boss and co-workers. If you haven't met your co-workers yet, be sure to do so before you make a final decision.□

No matter how dissatisfied or unhappy you are in your current job, you will be serving your own long-term interests if you help smooth the way for your successor when you land your new job. Why? It's the professional thing to do, and even more importantly, your boss, colleagues, and clients are likely to remember your efforts, which can result in positive references on your behalf and even future job tip-offs.

Follow these steps and you will leave your boss and co-workers with positive memories:

1. Be diplomatic in explaining the reasons for your departure. Even if your leaving has as much to do with your not liking the way your boss manages as it does your wanting more interesting responsibilities, it's better to focus on the latter reason. There's nothing to be gained by criticizing your boss or the company, other than the temporary satisfaction of letting off steam. If you have suggestions about how work systems or processes could be improved, on the other hand, putting them down in writing can be therapeutic for you and appreciated by your boss and management.

2. Don't leave without giving adequate notice. Two weeks' notice is acceptable if you are not in a management position or in the middle of a project that will be hard for your successor to pick up. If it's possible to give more notice, however, do so because it will probably take your boss a minimum of two weeks to find a replacement, who may in turn have to give his or her employer several weeks' notice.

3. Offer to help find and train a new employee. No one knows your job better than you do, so your help in developing a more complete job description and list of responsibilities than currently exists will be invaluable. You are also in a better position than your boss to identify qualified candidates who you may know through school, professional activities, or personal contacts. Finding potential replacements may also mean you can leave your job sooner without feeling guilty at leaving your boss in the lurch. Your willingness to spend as little as a day or as much as a week showing the new person the ropes is another gesture your boss won't forget. Putting together written instructions is another smart move.

4. Don't let your efforts sag. It's easy to let details slide when you know you are not going to have to deal with your current work responsibilities in the near future. But your lack of attention may result in a mistake or foul-up, which is far more likely to be remembered than your otherwise good performance. Make it a point to finish up work in progress, or, if that's not possible because of the complexity of a particular assignment, at least provide your boss with a status report and a list of things that remain to be done.

5. Attempt to mend fences. It's especially important if your relationship with your boss has deteriorated. You might say, for example, "We have our differences, but I want you to know that I have learned a lot from you, which I really appreciate." If you take the first step and are conciliatory in your tone, chances are good your boss will voice a similar sentiment. But more important is his or her new impression of you. Taking the same approach with co-workers or staff who work for you is smart; you never know when their opinion of you will make a difference in your career.

6. Be sure to say good-bye. It's easy when you like and will truly miss the people you have worked for and with or if your office is gracious and organized enough to give you a party send-off. Even if you are disappointed that no one took you out for a good-bye lunch, don't slink out the door without a word. Make the effort to shake hands; it shows that you are a professional with class. And do not neglect those with whom you did get along; it's not hypocritical to smile and wish them "Good Luck." □

REVEAL HOW LONG YOU PLAN TO STAY IN JOB?

If you only intend to stay in a job for a limited period of time, what should you say about it when an employer offers you a job? Select the answer that you would feel most comfortable with.

A: Nothing; there's always the chance that circumstances may change and you might stay longer.

B: Be honest and explain what the likely scenario is.

C: Don't reveal anything about your plans unless you are specifically asked.

The best answer could be A, B, or C. What really matters is which one best fits your personality and style. Most employers assume that you are willing to make a commitment of at least a year, if not longer—some will even ask how long you hope to stay in the position you are applying for.

If you suspect you may be out of the running if you reveal your plans, A is your best bet if you want the job. If, on the other hand, there is frequent turnover in the job, your employer may be nonplused by hearing your future intentions and still make the offer.

If you have to leave in a year's time, you can only hope that your boss is not the kind of person who will resent your departure and give you a bad reference. □

WHEN YOU'RE SURE AN INTERVIEW WENT WELL

DO'S & DON'TS

No matter how well you think an interview went, it's wise not to make any assumptions about what's going to happen next. These guidelines can save you disappointment and even financial woes.

DO continue your job search. Follow up on resumes and letters you sent out prior to your "terrific" interview. If you have other interviews to look forward to, you won't be as let down if the job offer you think is coming doesn't.

DON'T make any new financial commitments. Buying a new car, signing a lease on a more expensive apartment, or even investing in new clothes for the job is a mistake before you know you have a paycheck coming in. If it doesn't, you may have to return those items or be financially liable for purchases you've made.

DON'T get your hopes up too high. Even if an employer was so encouraging that he said, "I'm sure you're the right person for the job," know that anything from a decision not to hire now to the company president's hand-picking another candidate can happen. It's better to keep your hopes to your-self than to prematurely broadcast what may seem like an imminent job offer.

DO keep a stiff upper lip. Highly skilled interviewers often convey the impression that they are very interested in you. But asking beyond-the-basics questions and making comments about your appropriateness as a candidate does not necessarily mean a job offer is likely, although it may indicate that you are a serious contender. If you operate on the latter premise rather than the former, you are more likely to weather a rejection well if your instincts prove wrong.□

Q & A

TAKE PART-TIME WORK WITH NO BENEFITS?

Q: I'm looking for a full-time job, but the only offer I have in hand is for a part-time position with no benefits. I have only another six weeks of unemployment compensation coming to me. Is it worth taking?

A: Even if you bring home less because your part-time salary is less than your unemployment compensation, you have the peace of mind of knowing that you will have some income once your benefits expire. Also, a part-time schedule will allow you to continue job hunting. And there's always the possibility that once you prove yourself on the job, you will be offered a full-time position.□

Before you celebrate getting the job offer you've been hoping for, don't forget the final important item you must negotiate: salary and benefits. For those who are not used to haggling over money, the thought that your future employer is probably going to try to hire you for as little as he can should be a big incentive to argue for more. Even if you're experienced in the art of negotiation, you may not bargain as hard as you should because you don't want to blow the offer.

You will find the negotiating process easier and feel more self-confident about your position if you do the following:

DON'T reveal the exact amount of your current or last salary. Some employers use it as a justification for the starting salary they are offering you, which is especially unfair if you have been underpaid. What is relevant is what you are going to be doing in your new position. The way to get around naming a specific amount is to say your total financial package (which may include an anticipated raise or promotion and benefits in addition to your weekly paycheck) is in the low-30s, high teens, or mid-20s. Inflating your salary isn't smart; your prospective employer may be able to verify it with your current employer or know from experience that it's too high to be real.

DO find out the salary range of the position beforehand. You can get a good idea of what employers in the area are paying people with specific skills and job experience through a number of sources including: salary surveys done by professional organizations (and published in their publications); help wanted ads; employment agency counselors; and ex-colleagues who are now working for different companies. The more sources you consult, the more confidently you will be able to argue your case.

DO bring up the issue if your employer doesn't. You might say, for example: "I'm really pleased that you think I'm the best candidate, and I'm sure I can do a lot for you and the company provided the starting salary is appropriate." Then ask the employer what figure he has in mind; even if it's more than you had hoped for, it's best not to say so; you may even want to say it's less than what you had expected if you want to nudge up the figure.

DON'T be too effusive in your acceptance. Even if you are thrilled that you got the offer, try to keep your emotions in control; otherwise, the employer may realize that she can take advantage of your enthusiasm.

DON'T talk about what you need; saying you need a certain amount to live on is not likely to win any sympathy or extra dollars from the employer.

DO talk about what you are worth. Focus on what you are bringing to the employer—your proven accomplishments as a cost-cutter, productive employee, or revenue-generator.

DO assess how badly the employer needs you. Many employers drop hints throughout the interview process about how many other candidates they are seeing and whether many or few of them have the right qualifications. If not, you can always ask. The less competition you have, the better the negotiating position you will be in. If the employer indicates that you are hands-down their top choice, you will also have greater flexibility in naming your price.

You can also assess how in demand you are by pursuing as many leads as possible. The best negotiating posture of all is knowing that even if you currently do not have another offer, getting one that will pay you what you want is reasonably likely. Of course, if this is your first offer after months of job hunting or you cannot afford to be out of work, you will have to be more flexible about what you make.

DON'T give up too much too fast. If the employer raises his too-low original offer, you should not accept it just because you are afraid she will think you are being difficult. Most employers will respect your fighting for the money you think you are worth provided your rationale is based on research, not just on what you want—it's a sign you will fight on behalf of your company's interests once you are on board. If an employer indicates an amount is his final offer and it's still not acceptable, you might try asking for other mone-tary or even nonmonetary benefits—tuition reimbursement, flexible working hours, or paid time off to attend professional conferences.

DO be pleasant throughout the negotiation. Avoid using threats or acting sulky. If you are firm but polite, you are more likely to win concessions from a prospective employer.□

Q & A

SHOULD YOU ACCEPT AN OFFER WHEN A COMPANY IS UP FOR SALE?

Q: I have been offered a job at a company that is looking for a buyer. I am unemployed, but wary of boarding a sinking ship. What would you advise?

A: Just because a company is up for sale does not necessarily mean that your job would be in jeopardy if it were sold. Much depends on how economically viable the company is. What you may be walking into is a climate where morale is not high because employees are uncertain about their own future. If you think you can function well despite that possibility, it may well be an opportunity. If ownership changes hands, you may be regarded as an asset by the new management because your tenure with and loyalty to the old company is limited. So if the position itself is the kind of opportunity you would otherwise be happy to get, go for it.□

THINK TWICE BEFORE TAKING A JOB THAT'S LESS MONEY AND CHALLENGE

When you are offered a job that is a step down from your last one, you may be tempted to take it, at least until something better turns up. Before you say "yes," be sure to take into consideration:

1. How marketable you are. If you have just begun your job search and turned up this option with little effort, you may be able to find a job that is not a step down if you are willing to look a little harder and longer.

2. Whether it will be viewed as a career liability. If you are in a technical or professional area, future prospective employers may ask why you were willing to settle for less. Unless it was your only option and you were under great financial pressure to take a job, these employers may question your judgment and whether you are the right person for a higher-level job. If, on the other hand, the jobs you are referring to do not involve highly skilled work, you probably do not have to worry about what your next employer will think. You will, however, have to point to evidence that you are not a job hopper.

3. How long you can support yourself without income. Figure out on paper what your expenses are, and whether your spouse or parents can help see you through a longer job search. Until you know exactly where you stand, you cannot judge how badly you need a job.□

WHEN A JOB'S TRAVEL REQUIREMENT IS PROBLEMATIC

Q: I was recently offered a terrific job that involved being out of town one to two weeks a month. I'm a parent and don't want to be away from my children that often. Should I be frank about why I do not feel I can accept it?

A: You have nothing to lose and much to gain by being honest. It may result in the job being restructured if the company wants you badly enough. Or the company may consider you for another job with no travel strings attached. The liability of not being clear about why you are turning down the offer is that the employer will probably not bother contacting you about future openings.□

155

PUT FIRST JOB OFFER ON HOLD

You've just begun your job search, and you have the good fortune of getting a job offer. Even though it seems like a good opportunity, you're not sure because you haven't had a chance to size up how it compares to what else is out there.

You may be able to reserve your option, at least for a short time, if you play your cards right. When the offer is made, be sure to first communicate your enthusiasm for the position, the company, and the person or people you would be working for. Then explain that you feel obligated to go ahead with several other already-scheduled interviews or that you are waiting to hear back from other employers with whom you have had interviews. Ask whether there is any leeway in how soon the employer needs a decision from you.

Unless he needed the job filled yesterday, chances are he will be able to wait a week or two or even longer. Be sure to emphasize that you want to make a well-informed decision and thank him for his offer and his understanding. If you turn up a better-paying job at a less desirable company, consider going back

to the first employer and asking whether he can meet the higher salary figure.□

ACCEPT ENTRY-LEVEL GLAMOUR JOB?

Q: I have been offered my first job in a glamour industry whose starting salaries are not enough to live on in this expensive city. I want to take it, but I'm not sure how to make ends meet short of asking my parents to make up the difference. Do I have any other options?

A: You do, but first ask yourself a tough question: Do I really have the drive and interest to work in this field? If you feel you would be cheating yourself if you did not at least give it a try, then you should accept the job. One way to reduce your living expenses is to look for housing that's not in the city or in more expensive neighborhoods. You can save even more if you share an apartment or house with one or more roommates. The downside is that your daily commute will be longer.

Moonlighting is another option, provided you have the time and energy. A weekend bartending or waitressing job can help you make ends meet. If you have good word processing skills, you may be able to work at a high hourly rate for businesses in need of after-hours or weekend help (law firms are a good bet).

Keep in mind that you won't have to maintain a lean and mean lifestyle or a hectic work schedule forever; if you prove yourself on the job, you will eventually be rewarded with a higher salary.□

HOW HIRING DECISIONS ARE MADE?

When two or more applicants have the right qualifications for a job, it's often attitude and personality factors that cause an employer to select a first-choice candidate. Here are the qualities that can make the difference in your being that person.

● Enthusiasm. Employers want people who want to work for them. If you want the job, tell the interviewer that and mention three good reasons why you feel you could do a great job.

● Dependability. Employers want to hire people they can count on to show up for work every day at the right time; people they can trust to see a task through with good results. Cite examples of situations where past employers were able to rely on you.

● Willingness to work hard. As more companies big and small try to keep profits up and labor costs down, it pays to let an employer know that you're willing to do whatever is necessary to get work done—whether or not it's specifically your job responsibility.

● An easygoing manner. Everyone likes to work with people who are easy to get along with. If you come across as someone who is personable and, better yet, has a sense of humor, you'll be seen as the frontrunner.

● Resourcefulness. Employees who can figure out how to solve problems are highly valued by employers. So talk about how you have done that–and with what results–in the past.□

TAKING A JOB WITH A FINANCIALLY UNSTABLE COMPANY

Before you accept a job offer, be sure to get a handle on just how stable the company is by:

✔ Asking your prospective employer for an appraisal of the company's future.

✔ Getting your prospective employer's reaction to things you have heard or read.

✔ Consulting with people whose opinion you trust and who are in a position to judge the situation.

✔ Asking yourself whether you can work and thrive in a crisis situation. If you feel you can, you may be given opportunities that were unavailable in your last position and make a difference that could result in personal or career rewards.□

BEFORE YOU GIVE NOTICE, GET YOUR NEW JOB OFFER IN WRITING

Computer programmer Robert Snyder was days away from telling his employer that he was leaving to accept a new job when a snag developed: His boss-to-be had promised relocation money that the company refused to honor. "I would have really been in a jam if I'd given notice because I was acting on this person's assurances, which he was obviously not authorized to give," says Snyder, who ultimately decided against taking the new position.

The moral of the story: Once you have negotiated the terms of a new job with an employer, ask for an offer letter that spells them out. While the law says spoken employment agreements are as viable as those in writing, there is no dispute about what's in black and white, while there may about what was said.

Here's what should be in an offer letter:

1. Your job title, a brief description of your responsibilities, and the name and title of the person to whom you will be reporting.

2. Your compensation package. This should include your salary or hourly rate, bonuses or commissions you will receive (and the conditions under which they will be earned), and stock options. You might also ask for a description of how your performance will be evaluated and how often. In big companies, these procedures are often described in the employee handbook.

3. Health benefits. A brief description of what's covered by your employee health policy (major medical, hospitalization, doctor's office visits, prescription drugs, dental work, and coverage for mental health and substance abuse problems) should be included. It should also state what additional family members will be covered, and how much, if anything, you are expected to contribute toward your premium or that of additional family members.

4. Perks. Any benefits that are not part of your compensation or health coverage should be listed here. They might include: use of a company car, relocation and moving expenses, outplacement or re-employment counseling (in the event your job is phased out), and expense allowances.

5. A statement saying that the terms stated in the letter supersede all earlier letters and conversations, provided you feel the letter addresses itself to all the promises your employer made. The reason? You want a written statement as to what you both believe your final understanding is.

Another possibility is that you will be asked to sign an employment contract (instead of being sent an offer letter). Most are written in legalese that's hard for anyone but a lawyer to decipher, and protect the employer rather than you.

One of the biggest traps you can fall into by signing one is agreeing to a no-compete clause that may unfairly preclude you from working for a competitor if you're fired or choose to leave the company.

Your best bet is to have a lawyer who specializes in employment law look over the contract to make sure you are not agreeing to things you do not understand or have not negotiated with your future employer. An hourly fee of $100 or more may seem like a lot of money, but it's an investment that could make a big difference if your employer does not turn out to be the good guy he seems to be in the interviewing process.

If no one you know can recommend a labor lawyer, look in the *Yellow Pages* under the subhead "Labor Law" in the "Lawyers" listing.

If your future employer is not willing to negotiate points you feel strongly about (after having talked to a lawyer), think twice about whether you really want to work for the company. Once everything is worked out in writing, you can feel comfortable about telling your boss that you are leaving.□

SMART IDEA

FINESSE AN ON-THE-SPOT JOB OFFER

Most employers like to think or talk over a candidate's qualifications before extending an offer. But you could get an on-the-spot job offer if the employer has already interviewed a number of candidates and you're a clear standout, or if the job has gone unfilled for any number of reasons and the employer needs someone quickly.

You will be better able to judge whether the job offer is right if you have already gone on a number of interviews and have developed a good sense of the scope of the job responsibilities; the going salary or hourly rate; and intangibles such as the organization's "culture," what it's reputation in the business is, and whether it's viewed by others as a good place to work. If you have doubts about the job or the company itself and your financial situation does not require that you start a job right away, you might ask the employer how soon he or she needs an answer. If the response is "Now," you're probably better off declining.□

Q & A

DELAYED HIRING

Q: I have been offered a job by an employer I would very much like to work for, but here's the hitch: The department cannot hire me for several months when its new budget kicks in. Am I foolish to accept it and assume that I am hired? Or should I keep looking?

A: Anything can happen in several months' time, including budget cuts. There is no harm in telling your prospective boss that you would very much like to accept the job and ask him to give you a letter stating your probable starting date, salary, and description of responsibilities. If he is unwilling to do that, be forewarned: The job may or may not materialize. Even with a letter, which in fact is a kind of employment contract, pursuing such a case legally if the job offer is rescinded may not be worth it if you have not incurred any financial losses (such as selling your home at a loss to relocate for the job). Your best bet: Say that you would very much like the job and, in the meantime, quietly continue looking.□

CHECK OUT NEW EMPLOYER CAREFULLY BEFORE RELOCATING

When you relocate, you invest a lot in that move—financially, emotionally, and professionally. It's in your best interest to make sure that your new prospective employer and job are everything they appear to be. Here's what to ask and assess during interviews.

● Find out what the new job involves and what the chain of command is. Don't simply rely on what your prospective boss tells you. Make it your business to talk to the person who currently has the job (if that's possible) and the people on staff with whom you would be working on a regular basis. Their comments can be extremely helpful in putting together a complete picture of what the job involves.

● Determine how important the office or division you will be working in is (you don't want to risk it being closed down soon after your arrival). Do your homework so that you can ask astute questions about the relationship of the division you're interviewing with to headquarters and other divisions.

● Research how financially stable a prospective employer is. Reading the business pages of the daily newspaper, trade publications, or regional business publications is advisable. If you find troubling indications, ask your prospective employer about them. Even if the company downplays bad news, factor it into your decision of whether taking the job is worth the risk of relocating.

● Meet with as many people in the company as you can. A minimum of two interviews with your immediate boss and at least one meeting with "important others"—colleagues, management, and staff—is advisable to help you form an accurate impression of company culture and workstyle.

● Get assurances up front. Before you give notice to your current employer, terminate a lease, sell your home, and bid good-bye to your friends, get the details of your new job and relocation costs that will be covered in an offer letter from the employer, no matter how trustworthy the person who hires you seems or how reputable the company is. It's a protection you cannot afford to be without.□

161

WORKING FOR A RELATIVE

Accepting a job with a relative who owns their own business can be a good opportunity—or a dead end. Ask yourself or your relative these questions before you say "Yes."

✔ Am I doing this to avoid a job search or continuing one that has not yet produced an offer?

✔ Am I likely to develop the kinds of skills I can take elsewhere?

✔ Do I honestly have or feel I could develop an interest in the business?

✔ Can I handle possible resentment from other employees who know I'm related to the owner?

✔ Do I get along well with the family member with whom I'll have the most contact?

✔ Are there opportunities for me to move up once I've mastered a set of skills?

✔ Is the family member offering the job acting out of a sense of obligation or because he or she thinks I can make a contribution to the business?

✔ Will the salary allow me to live on my own or save the kind of money I could if I were working for another employer?

✔ Am I leaning toward accepting the offer because my parents or other family members are pressuring me to do so?□

Q & A

START JOB WITHOUT PROMISED OFFICE SPACE?

Q: My new employer—who I have not yet begun working for—has promised me my own office, but says I may have to share space with someone on much lower job level initially. I don't want to get stuck in office limbo indefinitely. Would it be smart to postpone my starting date until he can find an appropriate office?

A: You are right in thinking that you are in a much better bargaining position now than you will be once you are on the job. At the same time, you do not want to start off your new job on the wrong foot by making too big an issue of it. Your best bet is tell your new boss that you feel you can be more productive more quickly if you have your own space. And find out what steps he has taken to secure an office for you. If you have not yet agreed on a starting date, suggesting that you wait until he locates an office is not out of line; on the other hand, do not renege on an agreed-upon starting date.□

SMART IDEA

FIGHTING A BAD RECOMMENDATION

Some bosses know better than to say something negative to a prospective employer about a former employee. Even though it may be company policy to be tight-lipped, most managers are tempted to say something—good or bad, depending on their feelings—about the person. If you know that a job offer was contingent upon your references checking out and you do not get it, ask the prospective employer what was said about you—he may or may not tell you. If he does, you can dispute it, but do so in a matter-of-fact way. You may give him a perspective that could cause a change of heart. If not, you may at least get an insight into how to handle this problem when the next job offer is imminent.

You should, of course, contact your former boss and tell her what happened. It's possible that she did not realize her comments would cost you the job, and she might agree to leave out the negatives or give a better context for her remarks the next time around.

If your former boss does not care that his recommendation has hurt you and you disagree with his assessment of your job performance, you have several recourses:

● Write or speak to his boss about it. He's probably aware that you did not have the greatest relationship and may be willing to put pressure on your former boss to button up.

● Let the head of personnel know about it. Human resources departments are tuned in to the cost and trouble of slander and defamation lawsuits and may advise him to keep quiet.

● Get a lawyer to write a letter on your behalf. The threat of a lawsuit is sometimes necessary to get your point across. Check with the lawyer referral services of a county or state bar association for the name of a local lawyer who specializes in employment law or defamation suits—she's more likely to take an interest in your case and know what she's talking about than is a general practice lawyer.□

WHEN YOU GET A COUNTEROFFER

You tell your boss that you are leaving because you got a terrific offer with another company. She asks you what was so terrific about it; you tell her. She comes back with terms that are even better. What should you do?

Reconsider your decision. If you like your boss and the organization, it's a pretty clear-cut call: You stand to gain more by staying than leaving. Not only are you familiar with how things work, you have developed relationships with staff, colleagues, and managers —don't underestimate their importance in how easily and well you do your job.

If the counteroffer does not address a major issue (such as your ability to work independently or who you report to), try to negotiate those points. Your boss may be willing to accommodate you if you suggest solutions. If that's not possible, you're in the desirable position of being able to go with your original plan.

Should you accept the counteroffer, don't feel too guilty about reneging on your acceptance of the new job;

employers know that that's always a possibility. So long as you let the employer know quickly that you have had a change of heart (and why), he's likely to understand and can make the offer to his second choice.□

FEAR OF FAILURE

Q: I recently interviewed for a job that requires more technical expertise than I have. The employer, however, is very keen on hiring me and seems confident that I can do the job. I don't want to leave my current job only to fail in a new one simply because I don't have the skills. Do you have any advice?

A: You're perceptive for recognizing that you and the job may be a mismatch. Employers sometimes do have biases (that favor you) but that may also cloud their judgment of how good a fit the candidate and the job is. If you think you could acquire the technical expertise you now lack through on-the-job or formal training, tell the employer that you would be interested in the job if he or she could provide that. If, on the other hand, you don't feel you could get up to speed quickly enough to be able to handle your job responsibilities competently, explain your concerns. It's possible that the employer may be interested enough in you to consider restructuring the job or building in time for you to take over the technical aspects of it more slowly.□

CHAPTER 8

SPECIAL SITUATIONS

WHEN YOU HAVE A VISIBLE DISABILITY

A physical disability, whether it affects vision, hearing, energy level, or ability to walk, communicate, or perform small motor tasks, does not necessarily interfere with one's ability to do a job well. Still, some employers who have never hired people with a particular type of disability may harbor misconceptions or prejudices that may affect their willingness to hire you. There are, however, positive things you can do to promote your viability as a candidate.

1. Think positive. If you have confidence in your ability to work in a particular type of workplace and do certain kinds of tasks, an employer is more likely to think so, too.

2. Don't reveal your disability before an interview is scheduled. You may take yourself out of the running if you do. The Americans with Disabilities Act prohibits discrimination on the basis of disabilities in companies with 15 or more employees. But some employers do not know the law; others choose to ignore it.

3. Let the interviewer know about your disability before you arrive for an interview. Why? Because it's in your best interest to learn in advance information that may be critical to your gaining easy access to an office or workplace. You might, for example, say, "By the way, I use a wheelchair for mobility. Can you tell me where the ramp to your building is located?"

The second reason for mentioning your disability is that the interview is likely to go better if an interviewer is not taken by surprise. If, for example, an employer is not expecting your seeing eye dog to arrive with you, he may be distracted and not focus his full attention on you.

4. Project self-confidence. The best way to do that is by practice interviewing. The more at ease you are, the more comfortable the interviewer will be. You can get the employer to see past your disability more easily if you maintain good eye contact, smile, sound upbeat about life, and convey the impression that you're eager to work for that employer.

5. Volunteer information about how you would solve a performance problem related to your disability. Employers are allowed to ask whether you can perform the functions of a job with or without reasonable accommodation or ask you to demonstrate how you would do a particular task. Bringing the subject up first, however, shows that you have the employer's concerns in mind. If, for example, you have a visual disability, you can say that you use a special computer keyboard. If you already own the equipment, you might want to volunteer to use it on the job (if it's unlikely you'll need it at home). A smaller employer who would otherwise have to cover that expense would appreciate your offer.

Any positive information that you can relay about how your disability will or will not affect your performance is worth mentioning. Talk about your stellar track record in terms of school or job attendance, or how you effectively dealt with job-related problems in the past.

6. Don't feel obligated to answer questions about your disability that are not job-related. The ADA prohibits employers from asking any questions designed to elicit information about a disability before a formal job offer is made. But, of course, some employers will ask questions about how you became disabled, and how bad your health prognosis is.

It's probably least off-putting to briefly answer the question without going into any more detail than you feel comfortable with and focus instead on how you successfully coped with your disability. You might say, for example: "I became paralyzed after a skiing accident. But I was able to resume my education within six months and ended up graduating with high honors." Then change the topic by asking a question about the job or the company.

7. File a complaint if you feel it's warranted. If you have good reason to believe that you did not get the job because of your disability, you can file a complaint with your local Fair Employment Practices agency and the Equal Employment Opportunity Commission. Neither one requires your having a lawyer. (Keeping a written or taped account of conversations you had with an employer as well as any correspondence can be helpful if you plan to file a complaint.) As of 1994, 11.5 percent of the complaints filed under ADA statutes had to do with hiring discrimination.□

OFF-LIMIT INTERVIEW QUESTIONS: HOW TO RESPOND

Employers are prohibited by law from asking job applicants personal questions (about their age, marital status, health, or family matters among other things) unless such information is a bona fide occupational requirement. Asking a young person his or her age would be a necessity if licensing, insurance, or legal requirements mandate a minimum age as is the case with serving alcoholic drinks, for example.

Some employers, however, ask illegal questions out of ignorance or in the course of casual conversation. Here's how to handle some of the most commonly asked off-limits questions without jeopardizing your chances of getting the job.

Are you married or do you have plans to get married?

Although this question is more frequently asked of women, it is sometimes posed to men because employers feel that married men are more stable and therefore more likely to stick with a job. If you do not feel comfortable disclosing your marital status, try to address the interviewer's concern or ask a question to find out what prompted the question. If

the job involves travel, for example, you might say: "There's no problem with my being out of town frequently; in fact, I enjoy traveling." Or you might say: "If you are worried about my leaving the position prematurely, I can reassure you that if working conditions are as good as you describe, I will be a loyal employee."

If you don't know an employer's motivation in asking the question, you might simply ask: "Does my being married or not make a difference to you as far as this job is concerned?" You might get an honest answer. If you're the opposite of what the employer considers desirable (i.e., a single man instead of a married man), make a case for why you are still the best candidate for the job.

Do you have young children? What kind of child-care arrangements do you have?

There are a number of legitimate concerns that motivate employers to ask about children, among them your availability to do work-related travel and put in overtime. One way to answer the question, then, is to anticipate the employer's concern and speak to it rather than explain your child care arrangements. You might say: "I assume you are asking the question because there are probably times when you need staff to stay beyond quitting time to meet a deadline. I'd like to reassure you that I have the flexibility to do that." Such an answer speaks directly to an employer's need.

If you are not sure what the employer's underlying concern is, respond with a question: "Are you concerned about my taking time off in the event that my caregiver is unable to come to work?" You can then decide what and how much information you want to give about your child care arrangements you want to give.

What would you do if your spouse were relocated or got a good job offer elsewhere?

Employers understandably try to avoid hiring people they do not think are going to stick with them long enough to make their job search and training investment worthwhile. You can say that a relocation is an unlikely scenario without giving details of your spouse's employment or answer by reconfirming your commitment to your career and explaining how this job fits into your plans.

How does your spouse feel about your taking a job (with these hours, travel requirements, physical demands or risks)?

Employers often ask this question to determine how much of an influence your spouse is in your work life and

choices. The best way to deflect the question is to say, "If I'm happy with what I'm doing, so is she (or he)," or "I don't try to tell her (him) what's best for her (his) career, and neither does she (he)."□

LEGAL AND ILLEGAL JOB QUESTIONS CHECKLIST

LEGAL QUESTIONS

- Have you ever been convicted of a felony?
- Are you able to travel extensively?
- Are you a U.S. citizen or have papers that authorize you to work in the United States?
- Do you smoke?

ILLEGAL QUESTIONS

- Have you ever received worker's compensation?
- Are you HIV-positive?
- Is there any history of medical or psychological problems in your family?
- Have you ever been arrested?
- Where were you born?
- Do you own or rent your home?
- To what clubs or organizations do you belong?
- What type of discharge did you receive from the service?
- What is your date of birth?□

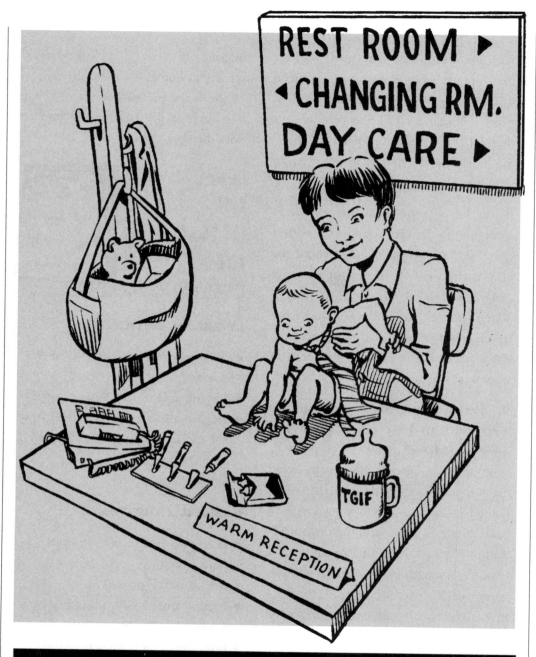

REST ROOM ▶
◀ CHANGING RM.
DAY CARE ▶

WARM RECEPTION

TGIF

IS THE COMPANY FAMILY FRIENDLY?

Q: I'm a working parent and sometimes run late in the morning or have to leave early. I do, however, always get my work done on time because I take work home and work through lunch. My current employer is very understanding, but how and when do I bring up the subject with a prospective employer now that I am job hunting?

A: First, you may want to do reconnaissance on this issue before you interview with a company. Find out from people you know who work there or by reading up on the company about whether its culture is the kind that is "parent friendly." That's not to say you should not consider companies who are not; an understanding immediate superior may be all that you need.

The answer to your "when?" question is: not until you know the employer is seriously considering you for the job or, better yet, has made you the job offer. Even if a discussion of working hours or overtime comes up earlier, it's probably not in your interest to bring up your need for flexibility unless your employer's needs are clearly in conflict with your own.

The answer to "how?" is: in a matter-of-fact, not emotional way that focuses on your prospective employer's concerns as well as yours. Explain why coming in later or leaving early is necessary and how you are willing to make up the time (or the work). One of your employer's concerns is likely to be the effect that your comings and goings have on others: You should try to assure him that your productivity and willingness to pitch in extra on occasions when your schedule permits should assuage co-worker resentment. Finally, if your new employer feels he cannot comfortably accommodate your schedule, know that you are better off waiting for one who can.

REVEAL SINGLE PARENT STATUS?

Q: I'm a single parent. At a recent interview, I volunteered the information, which made sense in the context of the conversation. But the interviewer looked troubled and began talking about the company philosophy of hiring stable, settled employees. I was told a more qualified applicant had been hired, but I think I blew it by being honest. If the issue comes up again, should I sidestep it?

A: Employers are not permitted to discriminate against you in a hiring situation because of your marital or family status. But some do, out of ignorance or disregard for the law. In the future, don't advertise your single-parent status. Instead, try to address what may be on the employer's mind: how strong your ties to the community are, how strong your attendance record was on previous jobs, your child care backup systems. You might even want to talk about how important you consider family values if you suspect that's the real issue. Stay away from divisive issues such as abortion, single parenthood, and nontraditional families, which may lead a small-minded employer to conclude that you're not cut from the same cloth as the other employees. There's room for agreement on subjects such as parental participation in a child's learning and life. □

WHEN INTERVIEWERS ASK...WHEN'S THE BABY DUE?

I t's a natural thing for people to ask a woman who is expecting, but it's inappropriate in a job interview situation. So is the question, "Are you pregnant or planning to become pregnant in the future?"

The Pregnancy Discrimination Act says that employers cannot discriminate against pregnant women in making hiring decisions. The problem is that most employers know the law and would give another reason for rejecting you.

If it's not apparent that you're pregnant, there's nothing to be gained by volunteering that information before you're offered a job. If, on hearing the information, the employer rescinds the offer, you would have a basis for filing a complaint with the EEOC (Equal Employment Opportunity Commission).

But if you're already wearing maternity clothes, you will probably be better off directly addressing the employer's concerns, which may include: (1) your inability to be at work continuously through a busy period because of pregnancy-related health problems or the actual delivery; (2) your deciding not to return to work after your maternity leave

expires; or (3) your asking for an extension of the typical maternity leave period.

If it's the case that your family depends on your income, let the employer know that that's the case. If you have successfully worked through previous pregnancies and resumed your responsibilities after the baby was born, you can reassure an employer that you intend to do the same this time around. It may also comfort an employer to know that you took off less maternity leave than you were entitled to because you wanted to get back to work. You might also mention that you fully expect to have a normal pregnancy and that your doctor concurs (or point to the fact that you have had no health problems related to pregnancy previously).

You might also suggest how the employer can get along without you during the time you will be out. Options include: your working part-time from home, training someone who can take over your responsibilities, or suggesting a qualified temporary replacement for yourself.

Of course, the bottom line in whether you convince an employer to hire you may be how in demand your skills and experience are. The closer they are to exactly what the employer is looking for and the harder they are to find, the better your chances for getting hired.□

FILING A COMPLAINT

If you strongly suspect that your pregnancy played a role in your being rejected for a job, you can file a complaint with the EEOC. You must be able to prove that:

- You are (or were) a member of the protected class.
- You were qualified to do the job.
- You applied and were rejected for the job.
- Someone with the same or similar qualifications was hired.

If the employer does not dispute these facts, you would win your case. But if the employer can articulate a legitimate, nondiscriminatory reason why you were not hired, you would have to prove that the reason was a pretext (fabricated to protect the defendant). If you were unable to prove that the reason was a pretext, the employer would be vindicated.□

Q & A

WHEN YOU DETECT BIAS TOWARD YOUR FOREIGN-SOUNDING NAME OR ACCENT

Q: I am a U.S. citizen, but English is not my first language. Although I speak it very well, I have an accent. I feel that I am being discriminated against because of my surname and accent. Is there anything I can do about it?

A: Unless you have evidence, not just a suspicion, of discrimination, you have no legal recourse. What kind of evidence is necessary? (1) You have been told by a company insider (preferably someone who is a decisionmaker) that but for the fact that you are foreign-born or speak with an accent, you would have gotten the job; or (2) you obtain access to a memo or other written document that essentially says the same thing. Suing an employer who did not give you a job can be costly and time-consuming. Of course, if you feel strongly about it, you should contact a lawyer who specializes in employment discrimination or file a complaint with the nearest regional office of the Equal Employment Opportunity Commission.

In approaching future prospective employers, remember that you will not get a positive reception if you have a chip on your shoulder or share your view that employers discriminate against foreign-born applicants. It's in your own best interest to be positive and upbeat and stress why your foreign background may be an advantage in a particular job. Advantages might include: your ability to spot market niches, provide customer service for foreign clients, or use your language skills to assist other employees or company customers.□

COME OUT OF THE CLOSET IN AN INTERVIEW?

Usually the subject of one's sexual orientation does not come up in an interview. Some interviewers feel it's a private matter or not relevant to the hiring process. Others don't ask because they know it's illegal to base hiring decisions on sexual orientation. (That's the case in eight states—California, Connecticut, Hawaii, Massachusetts, Minnesota, New Jersey, Vermont and Wisconsin—the District of Columbia, and about 125 municipalities.)

But if you are a gay man or a lesbian who wants to work in an environment where you don't have to hide your sexual orientation to keep your job, you should try to get a handle on whether it's likely to be a problem before you accept a job offer.

The trick is to find the right moment and context in which to broach the matter, something that's easier said than done. Saying too much too soon may be offputting to a normally sympathetic individual because he or she may wonder why you found it important to bring it up at the outset. Waiting until you have won over those who will be responsible for making the hiring deci-

sion before you ask a telling question is usually a reasonable way to go if you really want the job. Much depends, too, on your personality and style. Here then, are several ways to gauge whether your sexual orientation is likely to be an issue:

● Mention your involvement with a gay or lesbian organization on your resume or when asked a question about how you spend your free time in an interview. If you get called in for an interview, it's likely that your sexual orientation is not a factor in hiring or doing a good job in the employer's mind. Realize, however, that some employers may not call you in for an interview because you did include that fact on your resume. If an employer seems at ease when you answer such a question in an interview or asks appropriate follow-up questions based on what you say, it's generally a positive sign.

● Ask whether health or other benefits offered by the company are applicable to a same-sex partner. If the answer is "no," you might ask if it's ever been considered or whether it could be considered. How an interviewer responds is likely to be very revealing of the company's acceptance or intolerance.

● Bring up the issue directly by asking, "Do you think this company is a comfortable environment for an openly gay person?" It's probably best to ask this question of an interviewer with whom you have already developed a good rapport and who is likely to continue to support your candidacy.

What will make a big difference is how you handle yourself. The more comfortable you are about your sexual orientation, the more easily you laugh and joke with others, and the more unruffled you are by ignorant people and their sometimes thoughtless remarks, the more convincing you will be as a candidate. Managers who have never had to deal with such a situation before may have concerns about how your openness will affect other employees or clients. You should be prepared to address those concerns.

Of course, no matter how right you may be for a job and how carefully you have sized up the situation, your openness may cost you an offer. But avoiding the issue at the interview can result in dilemmas if you are hired. Should you later decide that you want to come out, or a situation comes up that makes it all but impossible to deny your sexual orientation, your working relationships may suffer because people may feel as if they have been betrayed.□

ARE CREDIT CHECKS LEGAL?

Q: I just discovered than an employer with whom I had recently interviewed did a credit check on me. Is this legal?

A: As of late 1994, employers can obtain credit information about prospective employees without advance permission. Employers are more likely to order credit checks when you are applying for a financial position or a job in you will be bonded. If the Consumer Reporting Reform Act is passed, employers would have to get your permission before hand. And permission could be requested only of applicants who would be handling large sums of money or items of great value.

Currently, employers are obligated to tell you if what they have learned about you in a credit report has adversely affected their decision to hire you and provide the name of the company that supplied the information. That's important because credit reports can contain errors. That's why you should request a copy of the information; credit reporting companies must supply it to you free of charge. If your credit report contained serious mistakes that you suspect may have had an impact on the employer's decision, you should send a copy of the letter and any documentation you send to the credit reporting agency to the employer as well and ask to be reconsidered.□

IF YOU STUTTER

Interviews are usually a nerve-wracking situation for most people, but if you stutter, they can be a nightmare because stress can make stuttering worse. If you follow these guidelines, however, you can make the experience more manageable and make a good impression:

DON'T try to hide your stutter; you'll get into awkward phrasing and your speech will be less fluent.

DO take your time when you stutter and maintain eye contact with the interviewer so that he or she understands what's going on.

DON'T apologize for the way you speak. Instead, talk about how stuttering has taught you things or equipped you to be more effective. You might, for example, talk about the ways in which it's made you a better communicator or sensitive to the needs of others.

DON'T hesitate to be funny or engaging, if that's your personality. If you show the interviewer through your attitude and behavior that stuttering isn't a prob-

lem for you, he or she is likely to recognize that stuttering will not stop you from doing a great job.

DON'T mention a severe stutter in the beginning. Otherwise, you may unintentionally make the interviewer uncomfortable. You might say, "I'm a person who stutters, so I'm used to challenges in life and on the job."

DO talk about what stuttering has taught you. It may be that you have learned to communicate more effectively or are able to work with a wide variety of people because you understand what "being different" is all about. Try to be specific or give examples.

DON'T misrepresent what you can and cannot do. If, for example, the job requires a lot of phone work, be honest and say that you have more trouble talking with people on the phone than you do in person. Likewise, if you have found ways to alleviate what is sometimes a problem, talk about them.

DO your best to come across as an animated and intelligent candidate. A journalist who decided he could do what he loved and stutter, or do what he didn't like to do and stutter, applied for a reporting position. The editor who hired him said: "I figured anyone who had the spirit to go into journalism despite his stuttering has the spirit I want working for me." □

BE DISCREET ABOUT REVEALING SUBSTANCE ABUSE PROBLEMS

STRESS BUSTER

Few interview dilemmas are more difficult than deciding what, if anything, to say about a past substance abuse problem. The Americans with Disabilities Act prohibits employers with 15 or more employees from asking questions about whether you have been treated for alcoholism or drug problems, since both are considered a disability. Employers may, however, ask whether you drink or currently use any illegal drugs.

You will have to decide what you feel comfortable revealing or hiding. It's important to anticipate the potential consequences of your answer and decide whether you can live with them.

Employers sometimes do ask the broad question of whether you have ever been treated for or fired as a result of substance abuse problems out of ignorance of or disregard for the law. (Their concerns include the possibility of a relapse and subsequent missed days, lower productivity, related health problems or your substance abuse jeopardizing the health or safety of others.) If you are asked a direct question, you have several options:

1. Ask how your answer would be relevant to your ability to perform the job, which puts the employer on notice that he may be asking an inappropriate question.

2. Say that the ADA prohibits those kinds of questions from being asked at an interview;

3. Answer honestly and stress the fact that you're now in recovery and in better shape than ever to do the job;

4. Talk around the question by saying what is now the case—that you do not drink or take drugs, are in good health and that you are confident of your abilities to perform the job.

If the topic of your treatment or recovery does not come up in the interview and you are hired, you may want to consider letting someone in management who is supportive of your hiring in on your secret. You should do so only if you feel a need to have someone know in the event that you do have a relapse and require subsequent treatment or time off. A second condition is that the culture of the organization not be so traditional that your revealing your past would jeopardize your job. One indication that your employer may be open to such news is the existence of an employee assistance program, which is designed to provide support to employees with mental and substance abuse problems, among other things.□

DO'S & DON'TS

YOUR HEALTH HISTORY

Mental or physical health problems can interfere with your being seriously considered for a job because the employer may fear that:

1. You will take more than your allotted number of sick days.

2. If your condition requires extensive future treatment, it may affect the company's health premiums.

3. You may pose a health risk to yourself or others given the tasks you are expected to perform.

Here are some guidelines to help you know how to deal with these concerns and insure that your condition will not be a factor in the hiring process:

DON'T volunteer information about an illness in an interview. Unless your condition would make it impossible for you to safely perform your responsibilities, there's no reason to bring up your history.

DO agree to take a post-offer physical examination or provide medical records. It's legal for employers to get or request this information once they have extended an offer.

DON'T mention that you have filed for or received workers' compensation. The Americans with Disabilities Act prohibits employers from making such inquiries because the answers may result in information about a disability. If an employer asks out of ignorance or disregard for the law, you will have to decide whether you think it's in your best interest to answer the question briefly or not. Of course, it never pays to misrepresent the truth.

DO talk about why you're now able to do the job you're applying for if the employer is aware that you had a past health problem. If recurrence is a possibility (or the employer is likely to think it is) it's probably best to bring up what the odds are—but underscore the fact that many people with your problem remain in good health for years or decades.

DON'T dwell on details of your illness if the employer is aware of your health problem. An employer is not supposed to ask questions relating to it until after an offer is made. But if he does, keep your answers brief and focus on why you are now able to do the work and perhaps why your recovery may make you an even better employee than you were before.

DO mention a positive attendance record if your illness is in remission and the employer is aware of your health history. □

WHAT HEALTH INFORMATION CAN BE OBTAINED IN A REFERENCE CHECK?

The Americans with Disabilities Act prohibits employers with 15 or more employees from disclosing medical information they obtained about you after July 26, 1990 (the date when the ADA was passed). So if you contracted cancer or were treated for a substance abuse or mental health problem after that time, a reference check should not turn up that information. A prospective employer could, however, legally ask a former employer how many days of work you missed, although he cannot ask if absences were related to a health problem.□

ADVICE FOR SMOKERS

Unless you are interviewing with companies who are smoker-friendly (a dwindling number these days), your smoking habit can interfere with your being hired. As the law stands now, employers have the right to choose between smoking and nonsmoking candidates and can advertise their preference by mentioning that they have "no-smoking" offices in a help wanted ad. The Americans with Disabilities Act, which identifies alcoholism and substance abuse problems as disabilities, does not provide the same protection for smokers.

In addition to the problem of having to accommodate a smoker by having a smoking lounge or allowing smoking breaks, some employers are reluctant to hire smokers because they think smokers develop more severe health problems at earlier stages than do nonsmokers. In these times of skyrocketing insurance premiums and health care costs, some employers feel that they can contain costs by hiring nonsmokers.

So what do you do if you smoke and you know an employer prefers nonsmokers? It's not in your best interest to lie and say you don't; if you're hired and the employer discovers you're a smoker, the employer would have the right to fire you because you lied.

Your best bet is to own up to the fact that you are a smoker (but only if you are asked the question) and tell an employer what you have done in the past or would do so that your habit does not affect others or your ability to do the job. If you confine lighting up to your lunch time or breaks out of the office, be sure to say so. And stress the fact that you are in good health and have not developed any problems related to your smoking.□

HOW TO TALK ABOUT A WEIGHT PROBLEM

Q: I am unemployed and 50 pounds overweight. I feel that my condition is standing in the way of getting hired because some people feel that a person who is overweight has no self-control and would not make a good employee. I recently joined Weight Watchers and am feeling better about myself. Should I let employers know that I'm in control of my eating habits and am participating in a program?

A: Definitely. By addressing this potential strike against you directly, you will probably increase the odds of the employer seeing you as a motivated and disciplined person.

Finding the appropriate moment to bring it up can be tricky; ideally, you want to wait for an open-ended question that will allow you to mention it casually. If, for example, the interviewer asks what you have been doing since you stopped working, give your answer, then mention your participation in Weight Watchers.

It's best not to mention your suspicion about employer bias; instead, talk about your personal reasons for joining: to feel better about yourself, to safeguard your health, to boost your ability to participate in physical activities, or to improve your appearance. □

SMART IDEA

WHEN YOUR RELIGION AND JOB VIE FOR YOUR LOYALTY

If your religious obligations are likely to affect days or hours when you can work, you should initiate the subject with prospective employers. It's probably unnecessary and unwise to broach it before an employer lets you know that you are a serious contender for the job. If you do, an employer may rule against you because your schedule is inconvenient. It's illegal to discriminate against a job candidate on the basis of religion, but it can happen, and savvy employers won't let you know that that's why they didn't hire you.

When you do bring it up, don't assume that the interviewer is familiar with the customs of your religion. You need only bring up obligations that would make it necessary for you to leave work early or take days off. Many employers give employees personal days to use for whatever reason they please. If that's not the case with this employer, say that you are willing to make up the time on other days or during busy times without extra compensation or take your work home. □

BE NEUTRAL ON CONTROVERSIAL POLITICAL ISSUES

Job hunters who have worked for a politician, candidate, or an organization that is active in politics are wise to avoid linking themselves with the views of that person or organization. Instead, emphasize the skills that you learned on that job that relate to the position you're applying for on your resume and in an interview. It's not necessary or relevant to share your own beliefs when you don't know in advance the views of the interviewer or firm you're applying to.□

Q & A

WHEN EMPLOYERS TELL YOU YOU'RE OVERQUALIFIED

Q: I have been unsuccessfully looking for work for seven months. Employers keep telling me that I'm overqualified for the positions I'm applying for. I really would like to have these jobs. Should I say I have less experience than I do to get around this problem?

A: Some employers will tell applicants they're overqualified when what they really mean is that they think you are too old for the job. It is illegal for employers to discriminate against applicants on the basis of age, but that does not stop some employers from doing so anyway.

You may be too old if you are in your twenties and applying for a job that is often held by a teenager or in your fifties applying for a job that is often held by someone a decade or two younger. If that's the case, downgrading your experience will not necessarily help.

Another possibility is that you are interviewing for jobs that do not require your level of experience. If you are truly overqualified, an employer may fear that you will leave once you get a better job, that you may not be a team player (because you must now do work that you once delegated to others), or that you will become easily bored with the job and do less than your best.

If you suspect you're overqualified, sell an employer on the fact that you're a "bargain employee" who can do more than what the employer expected. Express your willingness to get in the trenches and do the job that needs to get done at the salary being offered. A "can-do" attitude can make a difference in whether you're hired.□

LEGAL TO GET FIRED FOR JOB HUNTING?

Q: I was recently terminated from my job of four years because my employer found out that I was looking for another position. Is he within his rights to do so?

A: Unfortunately, the answer is probably "Yes." Unless you have an employment contract that specifies the period for which you will be working, a union contract, or a wonderful employee handbook, you can be fired for any reason that does not violate a federal or state law. Those who are most likely to be protected by law are employees who think they have been fired because of their union membership, race, religion, sex, age, or disability. Others who have legal recourse are employees who suspect they have been fired to keep them from getting their retirement, for reporting safety violations, or exercising their right of free speech. If your situation meets any of the above criteria, contact your union steward, your local Equal Employment Opportunity office, the American Civil Liberties Union, or, if you can afford to, a private lawyer specializing in employment matters.□

WHEN YOU LIVE WITH YOUR PARENTS AND ARE OUT OF WORK

DO'S & DON'TS

If you are living with your parents and out of work, you can stay on better terms if you do the following:

DO keep them informed about what you are doing and the results of your efforts.

DON'T spend too much of your free time doing nonconstructive activities such as watching television or playing computer games.

DO consider registering with a temporary agency or contacting employers directly about working on a project-by-project basis. If you're earning money and are able to help out with household expenses, your lack of a permanent job will matter less.

DON'T act defensive when your parents ask questions about what happened to a particular job lead or at an interview.

DO listen to and, when possible, take to heart your parents' suggestions about people you might contact or specific job leads.

DO be diplomatic if you have to ask your parents to tone down the intensity or frequency of their inquiries about your job search.□

SMART IDEA

DETERMINE ENTERTAINING "REQUIREMENTS"

Many jobs, particularly those that are in sales, involve wining and dining prospective customers in the evening or on weekends. If you hope to avoid that kind of duty, it's smart to raise the issue in an interview; you don't want to preclude yourself from a job opportunity by stating your limitations in a cover letter. Be prepared to talk about how you have been or could be successful without entertaining clients.

Make sure that the prospective employer doesn't get the idea that you are never willing to entertain, only that you want to do so when you feel it really will make a difference.

Even if an employer isn't convinced or willing to have a member of the sales staff deviate from what's worked in the past, know that you are making the right decision in finding out what the expectations are before you accept a job.□

BE HONEST ABOUT PRISON RECORD?

Q: Six years ago, I went to prison for selling dope. Since my release, I've worked at part-time jobs and recently earned my bachelor's degree. I'm afraid when I go to apply for a real job, no company will touch me because of my record. What I did when I was younger is over, and I'd like to be honest about my life, but how can I do that and still get hired?

A: Congratulations on turning your life around. You're right—it's better not to misrepresent your past, even if it costs you a job interview. But you'll need a chance to convince an employer that you're worth considering. Some job applications ask whether you've ever been convicted of a felony. You're probably better off leaving that blank, so that you won't be ruled out as a candidate before you have a face-to-face meeting.

When you do mention it, don't make it the first order of business. Do your best to convince an employer that you are a good candidate for the job. Present your employer with a list of references from your part-time jobs. The best time to bring up the subject is when you know the employer is going to do a reference check (unless he asks you a related question earlier).

Explain what happened briefly, say that your drug-dealing days are behind you, and emphasize the ways in which you have changed for the better. A progressive employer who is impressed with your qualifications is the most likely one to accept your past and make you a job offer. □

SAYING YOU'RE THE SOLE SUPPORT CAN BE A PLUS

Usually the fact that you are financially responsible for others is a positive thing to bring up in an interview because employers know that you are likely to be a dedicated employee. Before you say anything, however, it's a good idea to find out more about the culture of the organization. If you're divorced or a single parent, for example, your bringing up this information may put you at a disadvantage in a company where traditional family structures are the norm. □

GETTING HIRED AFTER FAILING AS AN ENTREPRENEUR

Q: After having worked several years for a prestigious employer (albeit in an entry-level position), I decided to try to make a go of a small business in an unrelated area. It failed, and now I'm back looking for a job in my former field. What should I say to convince prospective employers that I'm serious about sticking it out for the long run this time?

A: There is nothing wrong with having tried the entrepreneurial route—it's a goal of many working Americans. Still, an employer may wonder why you abandoned a chance for upward mobility with a known employer. Be sure to emphasize what was positive about your entreprenurial experience, while pointing out what its limitations were. If it was the case that people at your job level had to wait longer than their predecessors for advancement or the likelihood of promotions was decreased because of stagnation in the company or industry, say so.

Explain, too, what attracted you to starting your own business—your appetite for challenge or the need to see something through from start to finish. Even if the idea of being your own boss was a major motivation, it's best to keep that secret since you are now looking for a job that will mean reporting to someone.

In accounting for your return, you need not go into all the reasons why your business failed, particularly if they reflect on your inexperience or naiveté. It's probably enough to say that given the recession, your timing was off. You might want to talk about what you missed about working in your field and emphasize the reasons (beyond a regular paycheck) that you now feel ready to start again. □